伊芙‧馬洛 Eve Marleau——著 林柏宏——譯

令人垂涎的經濟與社會變革紀錄

品菜單 THE MENU

CONTENTS

前言

　　菜單有種與生俱來的誘人魔力 —— 它既是承諾，是邀請，同時也是一組指示 —— 不難理解為何法語的菜單「carte」一詞也指地圖。食譜教我們如何烹飪，菜單則建議我們該吃什麼、照什麼順序吃。菜單為我們規劃一餐飯的宴飲之旅，過程中也少不了引導和誘惑。

　　又稱供餐清單（bill of fare）的菜單（menu）在中世紀的烹飪書和手稿中就出現了，成為今日所見的模樣則得感謝法國人。儘管疲倦的旅行者自中世紀以來就在小酒館和旅館獲得住宿和飲食，但真正的「餐廳」—— 顧客坐在自己的餐桌座位，從菜單上的各式菜餚中挑揀餐點 —— 源於十八世紀中葉的巴黎，當時的餐館菜單有各種形式，塗寫在黑板上、由服務生大聲朗誦出來，或寫在紙上再交給顧客。十九世紀初的菜單通常以密密麻麻的手寫小字寫成，或是印在一大張紙上。到了二十世紀中葉，隨著餐館數量激增且競相爭取豪奢的顧客上門，菜單通常放在附有絲線、以皮革裝幀的小冊子中。

　　與其他史料文件（如信件、報紙、官方文獻和日記）相較，菜單較少受到關注。部分原因是菜單的內容通常即時且短暫 —— 反映當天或該星期的菜色，一旦過期就被丟棄。但是，歷史學家、檔案室和圖書館近來開始共同努力蒐集並整理菜單。菜單漸漸被視為內容豐富又複雜的資料來源，能夠從中得知可取得的物品和價格高低、技術發明、人的目標和期望、流行時尚與悠久的傳統。

　　菜單將帶我們穿越時空，回到幾十年或幾百年前、形形色色的過往時光。在這個各式美味兼容並蓄的大集合中，我們可以造訪皇宮，一覷俄羅斯最後一任沙皇的加冕典禮，或是透過學校的菜單重溫童年。一份又一份的菜單使人們享用的餐點如在眼前，生動描述著被長久遺忘的隱密內情，讓我們偷聽很可能發生過的八卦談話，因此有種讓人難以抗拒的魔力。有些菜單提

供了偷溜進私人聚會的機會，好比貓王艾維斯·普里斯萊（Elvis Presley）的婚禮早餐菜單裡，不但有香檳和牡蠣，還有滿足個人口腹之欲但非傳統慣例的南方炸雞。有些菜單則與某一歷史時刻的公眾政治密不可分。一九一八年，婦女參政運動者坐進倫敦密涅瓦咖啡廳（Minerva Café）裡享用了一頓四道式套餐，而選擇在素食餐廳用餐當時可是和爭取投票權一樣激進。本書匯集了各式各樣的菜單，對任何喜歡研究社會歷史、飲食歷史和外食用餐演進史的人來說，都是一場名副其實的盛宴。

波莉·羅素（Polly Russell）

LAND OF THE SKY.

Southern Railway Company

BIDS YOU WELCOME

COMPLIMENTARY DINING CAR SERVICE

ON OCCASION OF THE FORTY-SIXTH ANNUAL
MEETING OF THE AMERICAN ASSOCIATION OF GENERAL
PASSENGER AND TICKET AGENTS

ASHEVILLE, N. C., OCTOBER 15TH-17TH, 1901

FRUIT

MALT BREAKFAST FOOD

Apple Sauce   Preserves

Rolls

Coffee   Chocolate   Tea

BROILED POMPANO   STEWED OYSTERS

Raw Tomatoes

CHOPS   SIRLOIN STEAK   HAM

RAIL BIRDS ON TOAST
Fried Samp

BAKED POTATOES   FRIED SWEET POTATOES

EGGS AND OMELETS

SAUSAGE AND RICE CAKES

BREAKFAST

En route, October 18, 1901.

序言

　　從本質上來說，菜單是一份清單，讓人滿懷期待，展現創意，但歸根究柢，它也是一樣供人做選擇的用具。若以此角度觀察菜單，這些「清單」——一天之內在數不清的場合、地點被讀過無數次——可說是研究人類社會史最得力的工具之一。菜單讓人得知經濟景氣與否、政治演變狀況、科技進展狀態以及社會風氣。飲食是人所必需，舉世皆然，此一共通性讓菜單反映文化風俗的方式獨樹一幟，與其他媒體完全不同。

　　不過，我們認識的菜單是變化演進而來的，尤其是餐廳菜單。雖然最早問世的菜單應追溯到十世紀的古代中國，不過第一份印刷的供餐清單出現在十八世紀中葉的巴黎。當時的供餐清單遠遠稱不上營造氣氛、創造期待，比較像是粗略說明等一下可能會端出什麼菜餚、讓你和其他用餐者一起如家人般傳遞盤子共同取食。而且，早期的餐館並不被認為是翩翩上流、愛嘗鮮獵奇者或富裕有錢人的專屬領域，更類似離家遠行者歇息享受的空間，這種情況直到法國大革命才發生變化。歷史學家 L・斯潘（Rebecca L. Spang）在著作《餐廳的起源》（*The Invention of the Restaurant: Paris and Modern Gastronomic Culture*）中表示，當貴族聘僱的廚師們發現自己丟了工作，民眾外出用餐這項選擇才優雅登場，此背景下產生的新興中產階級有更多錢花用，更少時間料理家務，也更樂意讓他人為自己準備餐點。可以說，這是第一個得以從飲食相關紀錄一窺經濟和社會變革——此為菜單的核心歷史價值——的實例。儘管菜單在私人宴會中很普遍，但直到十九世紀中葉為止都是將所有菜餚一口氣端上共同享用的大餐桌，得等到十八世紀末和十九世紀初，每日菜色寫上了小黑板，不一定要點套餐而可以單點的「à la carte」形式才出現。時間往後快轉幾年，菜單的概念和結構變得更炫了。隨著十九世紀初高級飯店的

左頁與接下來幾頁的圖片皆為大英圖書館收藏的菜單卡和封面

MENU

NO COVER CHARGED
(AUCUN PLAT N'EST SERVI POUR DEUX)

COQUILLAGES ET HUITRES

COQUILLAGES		HUITRES FRANCAISES		HUITRES ANGLAISES	
		Portugaises	la douz. 4/-		
		Belon petites	„ 7/6		
		Belon supérieures	„ 9/6		
Bigorneaux	la portion 9d.	Armoricaines extra	„ 11/-	Brittany petites	la douz. 6/-
Moules Parquées	la douz. 1/-	Marennes vertes petites	„ 6/6	Brittany supérieures	„ 8/6
Little Neck Clams petits	4/-	Marennes vertes supérieures	„ 9/6	Natives Petites	„ 7/6
Little Neck Clams gros	„ 7/-	Marennes vertes extra	„ 10/6	Natives supérieures	„ 9/6
		L'Assiette Saintongeaise	3/-	Natives extra	„ 11/-
		(See full explanations on other page.)			
POTTED SHRIMPS	2/3			BOUQUET	la portion 2/6

COCKTAILS

		LE PLATEAU PRUNIER		FUMAISONS, CAVIAR	
Crevette Cocktail	2/6	Petit Sandwich de Caviar de Saumon		Truite fumée	2/6
Crabe Cocktail	2/6	Petite Coquille salade de Crabe		Saumon fumé	2/9
Langoustine Cocktail	3/-	Petite Coquille Moules au Curry	2/9	Caviar de Saumon ... la cuiller	2/6
Oyster Cocktail	3/6	Petite coquille, sauce verte		Caviar Pressé	3/6
		Fine Bouche de Saumon Fumé		Caviar Russe Sevruga (New Catch	7/-
				Caviar Russe Oscietre...(1939)	9/-

OEUFS

NOS SPECIALITES

Huitres Frites	les 3 2/6	Œuf en Gelée	1/9	Œufs Lucullus	3/-	Omelette au Caviar	3/9

POTAGES

Huitres Frites	les 3 2/6				
„ au Gratin „	2/6	Consommé aux Diablotins	1/9	Bisque de Homard	2/6	Crème de Maïs	2/6
„ sur croûton „	2/6	Soupe aux Moules	2/6	Clam Chowder	3/6	Soupe à l'Oignon gratinée	2/6
„ à l'Américaine „	2/6			Potage de Fruits de Mer	4/-		
„ en Brochette „	2/6						
Potage aux Huitres	5/6						
Variété Prunier (6 oysters)	5/-						
Potage de Fruits de Mer	4/-						
Clams à la Vapeur	4/6						

POISSONS

Le Poisson du Chef ...... See "TODAY"

ESCARGOTS DE BOURGOGNE 3/6

Coquille de Moules Rémoulade	2/-	Crabe Dressé Mayonnaise	3/6	Truite en Gelée de Chablis	3/3
Crabe à la Mexicaine	2/6	Petit Homard Rémoulade	4/-	Steak de Turbot Parisienne	3/6
		Langouste Mayonnaise	4/6		
		GRILLADE AU FENOUIL	3/6		
Hareng Grillé, Sce. Moutarde	2/-	Turbot au Four	3/6	Bouillabaisse	3/6
Moules Marinière	2/6	Sole Grillée	4/-	½ Homard Thermidor (1 per.)	4/6
Whitebaits Diablés	2/6	**GRENOUILLES MURAT** ½ douz. 4/6		Homard Grillé	4/6
Raie au beurre Noir	3/-	Pilaff de Moules au Curry	3/6	Homard Américaine	5/-
St. Jacques Prunier	3/-	Pilaff de Crabe Américaine	4/-	Homard Newburg	5/6
Truite Grenobloise	3/3	Pilaff de Langoustine Valencienne	4/6	Filets de Sole Prunier	4/6
		Pilaff de crevettes Newburg	4/6		

ENTREES, GRILLADES ET ROTS

Le Plat du Gourmet ...... "See TODAY"

Côtes d'Agneau	3/6	Pilaff de Volaille au Curry	3/6	Entrecôte Minute	3/9
Côte de Mouton ou Veau	3/6	½ Poularde au Riz Suprême (2 pers)	9/-	Tournedos Beurre d'Anchois	4/6
Rognons Grillés Vert - Pré	3/6	Poulet Maryland (2 pers.)	9/-	Filet Boston (6 Huitres)	6/6
		(Toutes les Grillades sont garnies Pommes Bataille)			

GIBIER

Bécasse Flambée	10/6	Noisette de Venaison, Sce. Poivrade	4/-	Civet de Lièvre	3/6
Bécassine Liégeoise	4/6	Canard Sauvage au Porto	12/-	Râble Lièvre, Purée de Marrons	9/-

FROIDS

Langue	2/6	Terrine de Lièvre	3/-	Poulet, la cuisse	3/6
Jambon d'York	2/6	Boeuf Mode en Gelée	3/-	Poulet, l'Aile	4/-
		Foie Gras à la Gelée de Porto	4/6	Mayonnaise de Volaille St. James's	4/-

LEGUMES

Haricots Verts au Beurre	2/-			Petits Pois à la Française	2/-
Endives Flamandes	2/-	Green Corn on Cob	2/-	Champignons Grillés Sur Toast	2/6
		Salade de Saison: 1/3 — Salade Panachée 1/6 — Salade m.c.b. 1/6 — Salade de Légumes 2/-			

FROMAGES

Cheddar, Cheshire 1/- Gruyère, Petit Suisse, Stilton 1/3 Camembert, Pont l'Eveque, Brie, Roquefort 1/6

ENTREMETS ET DESSERTS

Pôt de Crème; Chocolat, Vanille	1/6	Glace Vanille ou Fraise avec	1/6	Soufflé aux Marrons	3/6
Fruits Rafraîchis au Marasquin	2/6	Gauffrettes Bretonnes	2/-	Crêpes à l'Orange	3/6
Ananas frais au Rhum	2/6	Mousse Glacée au Rhum „ „	2/3	Poire Flambée à la Mirabelle	3/6
		Mousse Glacée Chocolat „ „	2/3		
		Coupe Jack „ „	2/6		

FRUITS DE SAISON

CAFE FILTRE 1/-   **CAFE DECAFEINE 1/3**   **Grape Fruit 1/6**

Open on Sundays for LUNCH at 12-30 and DINNER as usual – 7 p.m.
Starting from Sunday, 7th. January

"TOUT CE QUI VIENT DE LA MER — EVERYTHING COMING FROM THE SEA"

到來，歐洲和北美的菜單逐漸變成一種展示品，插圖裝飾之餘還提供多樣變化選擇，不再是一連串不得更改的菜餚名稱。菜單從此起飛，身姿百變，可以是創意拼盤，也可以是宣示道德意涵的載體。想想畢卡索為那間自己在巴塞隆納常常光顧的店作畫，以及一九六〇年代嬉皮運動中家喻戶曉的名人常常出沒的倫敦第一家素食餐廳。

但是，餐館之外的菜單呢？這些菜單通常可讓人更深刻了解政治與社會敘事。例如在德里，人們慶祝印度獨立紀念日的餐宴菜單就道盡了該國過去的複雜局勢，也許還暗示了將來會持續發生更複雜的文化認同問題（一〇一頁）。同樣地，一九四三年邱吉爾與盟友史達林、小羅斯福召開德黑蘭會議期間所舉行的邱吉爾生日晚宴菜單內容，也有某種外交展示作用，或者從微觀或宏觀的角度來看，呈現了極人性化、極微妙的權力鬥爭跡象。

若說得更抽象，「菜單」就是無論一開始多麼微不足道或如何激進猛烈，在全世界廚房和餐館餐桌上早已變得司空見慣的食物和飲料。要不是有 NASA 的科技讓人類及食糧能在太空中航行，兒時對脫水冰淇淋（dehydrated ice cream）的著迷或許也不會那麼浪漫。而且，不正是因為十九世紀初美國亨氏食品公司（Heinz）強力行銷，焗烤豆子現今才會在英國如此普及嗎？

在書中，我們將透過飲食探索長達兩百五十年的歷史，就像伴隨文字、琳瑯滿目的插圖一樣，這趟探索會發現的東西千姿百態。為了紀念今日已成典型的菜單形式，本書同樣分為前菜、主餐和甜點三大篇章。決定架構的前提相當簡明：在〈前菜〉篇，我們討論事物源起、創新表現和開拓者，從艾斯科菲耶（Escoffier）在麗緻酒店（The Ritz）開發出的革命性菜單到冷凍食品懶人料理如何引進美國中產階級家庭。這些因其與眾不同而存在的菜單分為三大類：首開先例、創新菜色和經典菜單（想搶先一讀請直接翻到第十三頁）。接下來進入〈主餐〉，我們會欣賞一些能夠反映或體現歐洲和北美歷史上重大社會與政治變化的菜單，從第一次世界大戰戰壕中的聖誕節晚餐到英國為小學生推出的免費校園供餐，再到第一本附彩色照片的食譜，這些紛然眾多的事件同樣分為三類：「創造歷史的餐點料理」、「催生菜單的社

會變化」與「料理書的歷史」。當然，最後必定要以甜點華麗收場，在這階段，歡欣氣氛更盛，但也不免令人悲傷，就像餐宴屆臨尾聲一樣。〈甜點〉這章的重點是繁華場、戲劇性和創造力，是那些具社會、政治或文化影響力卻消逝在歷史之中的富豪名流餐食、軼事或古怪的飲食習慣。在這一章裡，從末代俄國沙皇著名的豪奢宴會到海明威的經典露營菜單，再到尼克森總統在白宮的最後午餐，我們將一睹許多「著名的盛宴」、「藝術中的美食」和「最後一餐」。

雖然這些菜單都按時間順序分類與排序，不過我們並沒有任何線性敘述的意涵；這本書不是一趟企圖貫通烹飪史的艱難旅程，比較像是一些歷史片刻的匯集精選，希望引發讀者的興趣，娛樂大家並帶來驚喜。就像一份優秀的餐廳菜單，本書的目的是針對一些未知事物稍作介紹，對熟悉的事物深入說明，以及對經典老套做一些翻轉。如何將巴黎圍城期間貓狗成為伙食一事與貓王的早餐婚宴聯繫起來？從臭名昭彰的盛宴到「祕密」菜單，從戰時的茶几到總統的午餐，這裡的菜單無論彼此多麼南轅北轍，都具有其歷史意義。菜單似乎比擺在我們面前的下一頓飯要複雜得多，而且意義深遠。

STARTERS
前菜

餐廳菜單上的前菜具有兩項功能，首先是激發食欲，第二則是為主餐預作鋪陳。挑選有歷史意義的菜單時，我也希望達成同樣的功能。從馬丁尼調酒的發明和如今無所不在的速食快餐店，到溫布頓的草莓佐鮮奶油，以及艾斯科菲耶在麗緻酒店首次端出的菜色，本章重點介紹了這些領頭羊中的頂尖人物。

以下菜單不僅引人入勝，定義了社會和歷史背景，也介紹了後來成為經典的先驅。無論是使過往的奢侈品能夠大量生產（如今已成為司空見慣的商品）的簡單技術提升、實現交通移動中用餐的飲食革命，還是烹飪文化指標的最初化身，不同的餐飲演化長久以來持續至今，菜單都是其歷史起點。

Curry, Curry, Curry.

R. BANKS,

2 & 3, Green Street, Leicester Square,

SERVES A REAL INDIAN CURRY

Daily from 12 to 3.

Tennyson wrote of the " Cock," and
Their plump head waiter,
Where often he used to resort
At the hour of five by his indicator
To indulge in a pint of old port.

    I write of the Crown
Where men of renown,
To Banks' like good citizens hurry,
To lodge there their cash,
And receive not a hash,
But a luncheon of Real Indian Curry.

Friday, the Gt. Madras authority on Curry advises,

Thoom Curry Khana Koo Mungtha Banks Sab Ka
pass goue.

Wines, Spirits and Malt Liquors of the highest character.

Nov 5 1886

W. Straker, Printer, Ludgate Hill, E.C.

十九世紀倫敦一家咖哩餐廳的廣告單

首開先例

電影院的爆米花、下雨時海灘上的炸魚和薯條、農夫市集、路邊的炸物小攤，以及三道式套餐——有時候，習以為常的事物在文化上根深柢固，以至於人們從沒想過它們的來源。我們好好挑了一些菜單，看它們是如何、為何有助於塑造大家共享的社會發展。

DÎNER, 60 COUVERTS—SERVICE À LA RUSSE.

MENU.

Servi par six, dix sur chaque plat.

BUFFET SÉPARÉ.

Vermuth, Absinthe,	Canapés de crevettes (777)	Salade d'anchois (772)
Kümmel, Sherry	Gelée de canneberges (598)	Rhubarbe à la crème (3204)
	Thon mariné (831)	Radis (808)
	Olives (800)	Caviar (778)
Chablis	60 plats d'huîtres sur coquilles (803)	

POTAGES (3 SOUPIÈRES).

Amontillado   Consommé Colbert aux œufs pochés (225)   Bisque de homard (205)

HORS-D'ŒUVRE (3 PLATS DE CHAQUE).

Timbales à la Talleyrand (988)   Palmettes à la Perrier (922)

POISSONS (3 PLATS DE CHAQUE).

Haut Sauterne   Flétan à la Coligny (1168)   Filets de soles, Rochelaise (1276)

RELEVÉS (3 PLATS DE CHAQUE).

Batailly   Dinde à la Française (2029)   Selle d'agneau à la Chancelière (1739)

ENTRÉES (3 PLATS DE CHAQUE).

Champagne   Filets de volaille à la Certosa (1836)   Côtelettes de tétras à la Ségard (2259)
Pommery Sec

Homard à la Rougemont (1041)   Chaudfroid de cailles à la Baudy (2459)

RÔTS (3 PLATS DE CHAQUE).

Perdreaux truffés (2100)   Poularde au cresson (1996)

LÉGUMES (3 PLATS DE CHAQUE).

Château   Céleri à la moelle (2721)   Petits pois fins à la Parisienne (2745)
La Rose

ENTREMETS SUCRÉS (CHAUDS) (3 PLATS DE CHAQUE).

Brioches St. Marc (3006)   Pouding à la Benvenuto (3092)

ENTREMETS SUCRÉS (FROIDS) (3 PLATS DE CHAQUE).

Vin de Paille   Gelée aux fruits (3 plats) (3187)
Gaufres brisselets à la crème framboisée (3223)
60 Glaces variées (3538)

FLANCS.

2 Chariots garnis de pommes d'api (3632)
Une brouette garnie de fleurs sur socle (3638)

CONTRE FLANCS.

Deux étagères garnies de bonbons, marrons glacés et Victorias (3379)
8 Tambours garnis de petits fours (3364)   Macarons (3379)
Africains (3364)   Bouchées de dames (3376)

SEIZE BOUTS DE TABLE.

4 Corbeilles de fruits frais (3699)   4 Compotiers de fruits secs (3699)
4 Fromages (3697)   4 Compotes de pommes (3686)
Café (3701)

名廚蘭霍夫在一八九四年出版了《美食家》，此為書中的俄羅斯料理菜單

1808

巴黎的俄式上菜

　　如果試圖猜測依序出餐──每道菜先後端上，而不是一次全部擺好──的起源，很可能會有人猜是法國或義大利。有多少人會想到俄羅斯呢？

　　事實上，西歐菜單的雛形是一八〇八年到一八一〇年的俄羅斯駐法大使庫拉金（Alexander Kurakin）傳入巴黎的。庫拉金當時人稱「鑽石王子」，因為他的衣櫥精緻華美，舉辦的宴會更是無比奢華。由庫拉金主辦的晚宴一律採用俄式上菜，也就是一次為客人提供一道菜，讓他們好好品嘗每道菜的細緻、欣賞每道菜的專屬餐具，而且每一個座位上都有一張賓客姓名卡。當時的主流規矩是法式上菜，無論是前菜、主餐或甜點全部一起擺上桌，但當依序出餐的做法在上流階層開始流行，不意外，也隨之普及了開來。最終在十九世紀下半葉傳到了英格蘭，甚至被收入《比頓夫人的家務寶典》（*Mrs Beeton's Book of Household Management*，1861 年）。*

　　這份菜單是名廚蘭霍夫（Charles Ranhofer）在他的著作《美食家》（*The Epicurean*）中用來說明俄式上菜的範例。菜單裡呈現的這頓晚餐所包含的菜餚幾乎不可勝數，而且都是上流社會的餐桌上必不可少的，如魚子醬、龍蝦濃湯、松雞佐松露和糖漬栗子。

＊十九世紀英國女性雜誌出版商比頓（Samuel Beeton）之妻伊莎貝拉（Isabella Beeton）的代表作，書中介紹料理的方式為食譜建立了一套標準格式，並涵蓋了許多持家實務與社交禮節。

俄式上菜的餐桌擺置圖例，出自 J‧H‧沃許（J. H. Walsh）撰寫的《家庭經濟手冊》
（*A Manual of Domestic Economy*），一八七四年出版

馬霍姆德畫像，約作於一八一〇年

1810

英國第一家印度餐館

水煙筒

·

頂級阿拉伯香料調味的肉品料理

·

米飯

　　沒有印度餐廳或外賣餐館的英國城鎮現今可謂屈指可數。雖然印度菜的超高人氣和普及率無疑該歸功於一九七〇年代的孟加拉移民，但英國歷史上第一家印度餐廳卻是由孟加拉籍企業家、東印度公司的船長馬霍姆德（Sake Dean Mahomed）創立的，他還有另一個知名的身分：攝政王的理髮師。

　　一八一〇年，印度史丹咖啡館（Hindoostane Coffee House）在倫敦馬里波恩區（Marylebone）的波特曼廣場（Portman Square）附近開業，儘管自十八世紀就能在家庭和餐館中看到印度料理的蹤影，但印度史丹咖啡館卻是第一間由印度人擁有及經營的。在它供應的餐點方面，我們只知道為了迎合還不習慣這種口味的客人味蕾，菜餚中添加的香料不多，並搭配米飯上菜。一八一五年的《饕客尋味年鑑》（The Epicure's Almanack）描述，這間餐館的「菜餚用咖哩粉、米飯、紅椒粉和阿拉伯優質香料調味」，周圍有水煙壺的香氛繚繞。據說，馬霍姆德的顧客通常是從印度回來的英國人和駐紮在倫敦的印度外交官，儘管後者很可能吃不慣染上英式風格的家鄉料理。

　　可惜，這家餐廳在四年內就關閉了，不過這位烹飪先驅的遺產仍在，你甚至能在當時的餐廳所在地發現一塊綠色解說牌。

一九五七年，刊登在《人人》雜誌（*Everybody*）的炸魚薯條廣告

1860

約瑟夫・馬林的炸魚薯條

搗碎的鱈魚塊

·

馬鈴薯切片

·

豆子泥

　　現在的我們很難想像有哪座英國城市的街角沒有炸魚薯條店，但信不信由你，構成這個所謂英國文化象徵的幾項要素直到一八六〇年代才緊密結合在一起。雖然還搞不清楚是誰率先將它們組合起來，據信第一家「薯條」店源於大曼徹斯特區（Greater Manchester）的奧爾德姆（Oldham），那裡有一塊藍色解說牌寫著此地最早將馬鈴薯「削片」並烹調出售。然而，將兩者合而為一並入鍋油炸，一般認為是約瑟夫・馬林（Joseph Malin）的創舉，一位在倫敦落地生根的中歐猶太裔移民，第一家店開在斯特普尼（Stepney）的克利夫蘭街（Cleveland Street）。後來搬到堡區（Bow）的老福特路（Old Ford Road），由他的孫子經營直到一九六〇年代。

　　炸魚最有可能是十八世紀後期從葡萄牙猶太人社區傳入的 —— 甚至曾出現在狄更斯（Charles Dickens）的作品中，如《孤雛淚》（*Oliver Twist*）和《雙城記》（*A Tale of Two Cities*），而以這種方式製作馬鈴薯幾乎可以肯定是愛爾蘭人的發明。然而若談到配菜，近年來不同地域的偏好發揮了重要作用。在英格蘭北部和中段米德蘭地區（the Midlands），豌豆泥最受歡迎，咖哩醬和肉汁也有人氣。想特別提醒的是，如果在英國南部點炸魚薯條，就要有吃到炸魚帶魚皮的心理準備 —— 這種倫敦北部的做法總讓某些人不滿。

TOUR OF THE PRESIDENT THROUGH THE NORTHWEST.

Breakfast

FRESH FRUIT

ROLLED OATS WITH CREAM

BROILED FRESH MACKEREL

SIRLOIN STEAK, PLAIN, MUSHROOMS OR TOMATO SAUCE

HAM   BREAKFAST BACON

LAMB CHOPS

FRIED COUNTRY SAUSAGE

BROILED TEAL DUCK

EGGS—   BOILED   FRIED   SCRAMBLED

OMELETTES—PLAIN, WITH HAM, PARSLEY, JELLY OR RUM

POTATOES—   BAKED   FRIED   STEWED IN CREAM

GREEN TEA   ENGLISH BREAKFAST TEA

COFFEE   MILK   COCOA

GRIDDLE CAKES, MAPLE SYRUP

CORN MUFFINS   TOAST   HOT ROLLS

Pullman Dining Car Service.
En Route, September 21, 1902.

一九〇二年九月二十一日，普爾曼公司餐車提供的「總統西北行旅」
（Tour of the President Through the Northwest）早餐菜單

1868

在火車上用餐

一八〇〇年代在交通工具上用餐的情況與我們今天生活的世界相差甚遠，沒有縮小的塑膠酒瓶，也沒有包裝小巧的三明治。當時在火車上用餐不僅出於實際考量，避免為了吃飯停車而拉長旅行時間，還必須考慮到用餐體驗是否優雅合宜。

「餐車車廂」（dining car）的概念由美國火車製造商普爾曼公司（Pullman Company）於一八六八年提出。在此之前，長途旅行必須停靠道路休息站，而休息站僅提供簡易的食品和飲料，將價格和實用性放在首位，稱不上享受。不久之後，餐車車廂在全美國所有主要路線上開始營運，推出的服務一代比一代豪華。

英國直到一八七九年才開始在火車上供餐，當時一列從底特律進口的普爾曼供餐列車行駛在倫敦國王十字站（London King's Cross）和里茲站（Leeds）之間的大北方鐵路（Great Northern Railway）上，而且毫無疑問地保證提供一流的服務。根據《倫敦新聞畫報》（*Illustrated London News*）報導，所有佳餚都由廚師現場準備，整輛車廂包含了「居中的沙龍餐廳，後面的廚房和前頭的吸菸室，以及管家的儲物間、女士更衣室、男士洗手間、櫥櫃和火爐」。

回美國來看一看這份奢華的早餐菜單吧，專為老羅斯福總統（Theodore Roosevelt）競選造勢的西北之旅供應，這是他為共和黨候選人催票的行程。從菜單中可見普爾曼公司如何在大西洋兩岸都推出高級服務，有現煎現做的沙朗牛排、雞蛋、鴨肉和淋上楓糖漿的美式鬆餅。

GREAT NORTHERN RAILWAY

DINING CAR SERVICE

英國大北方鐵路餐車的菜單

約一八七七年至一八七九年間美國太平洋鐵路的餐車車廂一景，
圖片來自盧卡斯（Charles Lucas）的私人收藏

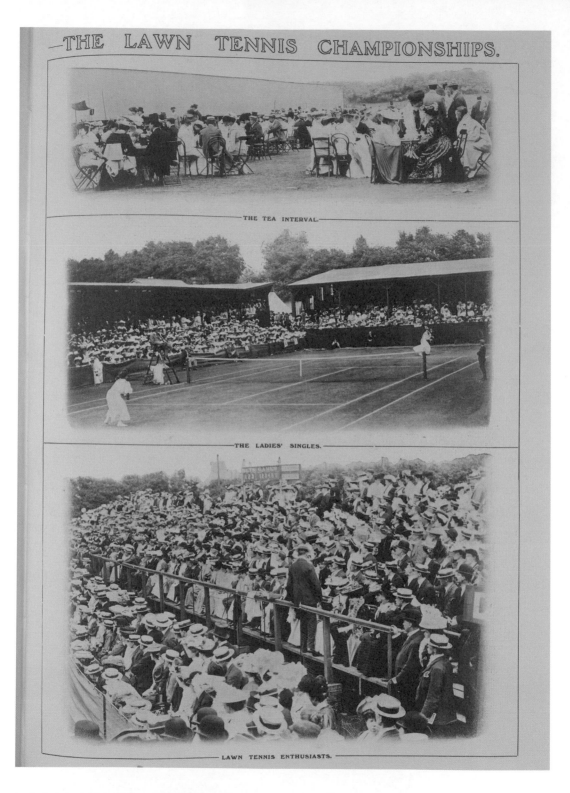

一九〇九年六月十六日，《王與國》雜誌（*Throne and Country* magazine）
的溫布頓網球賽報導

1877

當網球遇上草莓佐鮮奶油

皮姆酒

·

小黃瓜三明治

·

草莓佐鮮奶油

　　比起如今常和它聯想在一起的那項英國體育賽事，草莓佐鮮奶油這對經典組合的出現可要早得多了。

　　草莓佐鮮奶油是都鐸王朝宴會餐桌上的固定班底，據說十六世紀早期在漢普頓宮（Hampton Court Palace）廚房裡製作後才開始流行起來。

　　很多討論圍繞著這道餐點本身，但關於草莓佐鮮奶油如何在溫布頓球賽觀眾之間變成搶手貨，還沒什麼人說得出確切的細節。

　　第一屆溫布頓網球錦標賽於一八七七年舉行，根據幾位飲食史學家的說法，當時草莓是一種非常時髦的奢侈品，七月初是生產旺季，而所有證據都表明，首屆比賽在場至少兩百位參加者都曾接受招待，享用這道甜點。

　　時間快轉到一九五四年，《考文垂電訊晚報》（*Coventry Evening Telegraph*）一篇文章讚嘆道，溫布頓賽事過去五十年來受歡迎的程度和伴隨的魅力如何遽增，文中所舉的例子像是「無處不在的採訪記者」和「場外草坪上的草莓佐鮮奶油下午茶」。無論一開始是怎麼來的，草莓佐鮮奶油這道甜點已經和溫布頓網球賽密不可分，光是二〇一七年賽事期間就吃掉了三十三噸草莓。

一九五七年，吉百利巧克力刊登在《人人》雜誌上的牛奶托盤系列廣告

1915

盒裝巧克力之起伏盛衰

完美果仁糖

·

榛果旋風

·

草莓誘惑

·

香甜萊姆

·

異國情調

　　很難想像這款英國最著名的巧克力盒，一九六八年到二〇〇三年間的盒身上並沒有它最具代表性的「牛奶托盤勇士」（Milk Tray Man）圖樣。吉百利（Cadbury）早從一九一五年開始就一直生產這款巧克力精選禮盒。

　　這款巧克力盒的名稱源於當時向顧客展售巧克力的方式；巧克力排列在托盤上，可散裝出售，選好後再裝入盒子裡——透露出某種奢華，又顯得與眾不同。吉百利預先選好不會過重、約半磅的巧克力，並以托盤展示的形式亮相，再配上漂亮的紫色包裝，推出後立即大受歡迎。巧克力雖屬放縱享樂，對中產階級來說價格卻相對親民，因此成為社交場合的送禮首選。

　　到了一九三〇年代中期，「牛奶托盤」（Milk Tray）成為英國最受歡迎的巧克力盒，能與之匹敵的只有競爭對手朗特里（Rowntree）的「黑魔法」（Black Magic）系列。

　　隨著時間流逝，口味也隨之調整，但完美果仁糖、榛果旋風和草莓誘惑等暢銷經典款始終存在。當然，經典不只這三款，可惜像是香甜萊姆與異國情調（吉百利對土耳其軟糖的改造）等口味已經找不到了。

一九三五年左右，伊斯特本（Eastbourne）婦女協會市集上一整筐的農產品

1919

婦女協會的農夫市集

當令食蔬
·
維多利亞海綿蛋糕
·
杏桃果仁塔

　　婦女協會（Women's Institute，簡稱 WI 更廣為人知）有著獨特魅力，它既是過往的標誌，現今和將來也仍繼續發揮著至關重要的作用。這個由社區領導的組織一九一五年在英國成立之初，目的是為陷入一戰深淵的農村地區重新注入能量，在徵兵吸走人力的時期鼓勵婦女生產糧食，維持農業運作。為了達到此一目的，其中一項做法是由婦女協會發起地方市集，讓婦女們將自家菜園和小農地中收穫的農產品帶來，把多餘的食物轉售給當地社區。

　　第一個地方市集於一九一九年在東薩塞克斯郡（East Sussex）的首府劉易斯（Lewes）舉行，在產物最豐盛的高峰時期，攤位多達二十三個。擺攤者販賣了包含當令蔬菜和花卉、雞蛋、奶油、鮮奶油、蛋糕、果醬和蜜餞漬物等各種產品，都由自家小農場生產，最終這項活動也開放給當地農民和退役軍人參加。當時最受歡迎的餐點包括維多利亞海綿蛋糕、杏桃果仁塔和水果蛋糕。

　　《西薩塞克斯郡公報》（*West Sussex Gazette*）稱這項活動是「年輕女性的好機會」，在大蕭條和第二次世界大戰期間及往後的日子裡，該計畫持續支援著當地經濟，說它是整個社區的好機緣也不為過。

美國，在小賣部買零食的男人，照片年代日期不明

1930

零食搶進美國電影院

爆米花
·
汽水
·
糖果餅乾

如今，爆米花在世界各地都與電影形影不離，但我們看電影時吃零食不太是為了填飽肚子，背後原因比較可能是一九三〇年代美國經濟大蕭條期間，戲院主人能藉此獲得經濟利益。

一八九五年，電影界教父盧米埃兄弟（the Lumière brothers）在巴黎向付費觀眾播放了史上第一部「電影」，爆米花則一直等到約三十年後才出現。

直到一九二〇年代中期，所有電影都是附有字幕的無聲默片，現場不僅靜得似乎連一根針掉在地上都聽得見，由於下層階級的識字率不高，字幕也妨礙了多數人專心欣賞影像。

隨著所謂「有聲電影」出現，電影突然變得好懂許多，電影院也生意興隆。但是，經濟不景氣使娛樂活動受到重創。當時在美國，爆米花已經是一種相當受歡迎的小吃，電影院老闆們於是想到了這種投資成本不高又能增加利潤的方法。如此一來，無論是過道上的個人小販賣的還是門廳的小賣部販售的零食，爆米花、汽水和糖果餅乾都變成了觀影經驗的重要元素。

APPETISERS

1. Mixed Appetiser (Served 2) £7.50
   (Includes Spare Ribs, Seaweed, Sesame Prawn
   on Toast, Spring Rolls & Fried Chicken Wings)
2. Spare Ribs in BBQ sauce £4.80
3. Spare Ribs with Spices & Chilli 🌶£4.80
4. Capital Spare Ribs with
   Fruity Sauce...................................£4.80
5. Dry Spare Ribs (Served with Lemon) £4.80
6. Deep Fried Chicken with
   Spices & Chilli 🌶 £4.20
7. Deep Fried Chicken Wings with
   Sweet Chilli Dip (6) 🌶....................£3.60
8. Butterfly King Prawns with
   Breadcrumbs.................................£4.80
9. Sesame Prawn on Toast................£2.80
10. Crispy King Prawns with
    Spices & Chilli 🌶 £4.80
11. Crispy Squid with Spices & Chilli 🌶£4.80
12. Grilled Dumplings (4) £3.00
    (Vinegar & Ginger Dip)
13. Satay Chicken with
    Peanut Sauce (3 skewers) £3.60
14. Satay Beef with Peanut Sauce ...£3.80
    (3 skewers)
15. Crispy Seaweed...........................£3.00
16. Crispy Won Ton with
    Sweet & Sour Sauce.....................£3.00
17. Spring Rolls (2) £2.20
18. Mini Vegetable Spring Rolls (8) ...£2.00
19. Vegetable Samosas (8) £2.00
20. Prawn Crackers............................£1.50
21. Crispy Aromatic Duck ...... Quarter £7.50
    (Served with Pancakes,............. Half £13.50
    Cucumber, Spring Onions & Hoisin Sauce)
22. Crispy Pork...................................£6.00
    (Served with Pancakes, Cucumber,
    Spring Onions & Hoisin Sauce)

SOUPS

23. Chicken & Sweetcorn Soup £2.00
24. 'Crabmeat' & Sweetcorn Soup....£2.20
25. Chicken & Noodle Soup...............£2.00
26. Chicken & Mushroom Soup £2.00
27. Mixed Vegetable Soup.................£2.00
28. Hot & Sour Soup..........................£2.20
29. 'Tom Yum' Thai Prawn Soup.......£2.50
30. 'Tom Yum' Thai Chicken Soup £2.50

CHICKEN DISHES

31. Crispy Shredded Chicken with Chilli Sauce 🌶🌶 ... £4.50
32. Chicken with Cashew Nuts.......................£4.50
33. Chicken 'Chinese Style' (with a Bed of Beansprouts).. £4.20
34. Chicken with Ginger & Spring Onions £4.20
35. Chicken with Mushrooms.........................£4.20
36. Chicken with Green Peppers &
    Black Bean Sauce 🌶................................£4.20
37. Chicken with Mushrooms & Black Bean Sauce 🌶£4.20
38. Chicken with Bamboo Shoots &
    Water Chestnuts £4.20
39. Chicken with Pineapple............................£4.20
40. Chicken in Satay Sauce 🌶........................£4.20
41. Chicken 'Szechuan Style' 🌶🌶..................£4.20
42. Chicken in Lemon Sauce..........................£4.20
43. Kung Po Chilli Chicken 🌶🌶......................£4.20

DUCK DISHES

44. Roast Duck 'Chinese' Style........................£4.80
    (with a Bed of Beansprouts)
45. Duck with Cashew Nuts.............................£4.80
46. Duck with Ginger & Spring Onions £4.80
47. Duck with Mushrooms in Oyster Sauce...........£4.80
48. Duck with Green Peppers &
    Black Bean Sauce 🌶................................£4.80
49. Duck with Pineapple.................................£4.80
50. Duck in Orange Sauce..............................£4.80
51. Duck in Plum Sauce £4.80

MEAT DISHES

52. Crispy Shredded Beef with Chilli Sauce 🌶🌶 ......£4.50^^
53. Beef with Cashew Nuts.............................£4.30
54. Beef with Ginger and Spring Onions £4.20
55. Beef with Mushrooms in Oyster Sauce..............£4.20
56. Beef with Green Peppers & Black Bean Sauce 🌶£4.20
57. Beef with Mushrooms & Black Bean Sauce 🌶 £4.20
58. Beef in Satay Sauce 🌶.............................£4.20
59. Beef 'Szechuan Style' 🌶🌶.......................£4.20
60. Beef with Tomato £4.20
61. Lamb with Ginger & Spring Onions £4.70
62. Lamb with Green Peppers &
    Black Bean Sauce 🌶................................£4.70

英國彼得伯勒（Peterborough）的喜樂屋外賣（Lucky House Takeaway），
照片年代日期不明

1958

周六夜外賣餐

糖醋雞丁

·

什錦雜碎

·

薯條

英國人對中式餐點有著深厚的感情，此情感據說可追溯到十九世紀末，當時由於航海貿易興盛，利物浦和倫敦等港口城市開始有餐館和超市營業。一九一〇年左右，英國第一條「唐人街」出現在倫敦東區的萊姆豪斯（Limehouse）。

二戰後，中餐館的數量開始穩步增長。首先是由於從香港來的人們遷入，其次是因為英國政府反對毛澤東共產政權的立場導致中國使館的工作人員滯留在英國首都。但是一直到一九五八年，外賣中餐的概念才誕生。

有一種說法是這樣的，鄭冠（Zung Koon 音譯）是倫敦最早的中餐館老闆之一，他兒子在倫敦西邊的貝斯沃特（Bayswater）開設了蓮花小館（The Lotus House），由於供應的餐點深受顧客喜愛，得不到座位內用的人便要求外帶回家。

此時的菜單早已經過很大的調整以符合英國人的口味，內容包含了傳統英國菜單中所有的顧客心頭好，例如牛排、煎蛋、薯條，甚至是混合燒烤，但也供應什錦雜碎（chop suey，一種符合西方胃口的麵條料理）、糖醋雞丁和糖醋豬肉。由於營業時間到晚上十一點三十分左右（此時酒吧都已關門），又提供價格實惠的食物，中餐館和外賣店很快就在全英國各地興起。

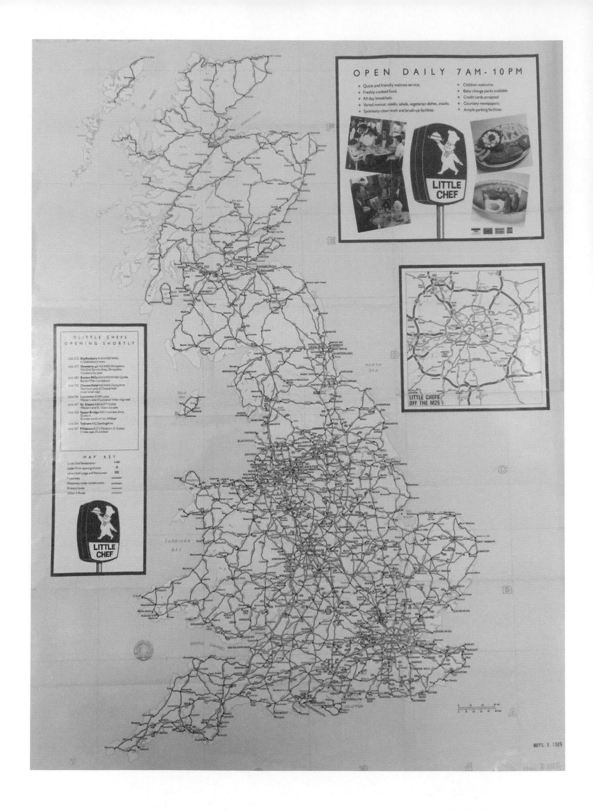

一九八七年，高速公路上的小廚師連鎖店分布圖

1958

「小廚師」如何擄獲大家的心

焗豆吐司

·

醃豬後腿肉佐雞蛋和鳳梨

·

水果雞尾酒加冰淇淋

　　一九五八年開業的英國連鎖公路餐廳「小廚師」（Little Chef）就像美國的速食連鎖店一樣反映了社會趨勢的變化。各地鋪設高速公路、雙薪家庭增加、人們旅行時追求便利，這些都為連鎖餐飲業的擴張帶來了完美的巨變契機。儘管此時公路旅館已經存在了數百年，「小餐館」的概念卻是「小廚師」老闆阿爾珀（Sam Alper）從美國帶回來的，並在往後十年內，於全英國 A 級主幹公路上開設了二十五間分店。

　　「小廚師」曾經有好一陣子沒什麼競爭對手，麥當勞直到一九七四年才在英國開設第一家店，隨後是一九七六年的漢堡王。在初始階段，麥當勞和漢堡王都沒有試圖開發旅行者客群。

　　事實上，第一家「小廚師」餐廳開設在雷丁（Reading）郊外的一輛露營拖車上。阿爾珀以前是飛燕（Sprite）露營車的設計者兼製造商，這份工作讓他看到了商機，發現供餐餵飽旅行度假的家庭有賺頭。「小廚師」的早期菜單包括「旅人的小吃」，如起司漢堡、焗豆吐司、醃豬後腿肉佐雞蛋和鳳梨、肝片配培根和洋蔥、鍋煎牛排佐洋蔥圈和薯片，還有甜點 —— 水果雞尾酒加冰淇淋和鬆餅加糖漬葡萄乾。產品中最具代表性的、充滿櫻桃和香草冰淇淋的「歡樂」鬆餅於一九七六年首次出現在菜單上，同樣受歡迎的「奧林匹克」早餐 —— 培根、香腸、雞蛋、蘑菇、炒馬鈴薯、烤番茄、馬鈴薯煎餅、焗豆子和炸麵包 —— 則是一九九四年推出的。

　　儘管「小廚師」榮光不再，最後一家店已於二〇一八年關閉，但每當聽見「我們快到了嗎？」這句話，總會想起這間具有歷史意義的公路餐廳。

1 Double-Double, French Fries, and Medium Drink $7⁷⁶⁰ +tax

2 Cheeseburger, French Fries, and Medium Drink $6⁴⁰ +tax

3 Hamburger, French Fries, and Medium Drink $6¹⁰ +tax

Fresh

DOUBLE-DOUBLE®
Double Meat
Double Cheese
$3⁹⁵

CHEESEBURGER $2⁷⁵

HAMBURGER $2⁴⁵

Fresh
FRENCH FRIES $1⁸⁵

SHAKES
Chocolate
Strawberry
Vanilla
$2⁵⁰

NUTRITION INFORMATION AVAILABLE UPON REQUEST

COKE *Classic or Diet*			
ROOT BEER			
DR PEPPER			
SEVEN-UP			
LEMONADE *Pink or Light*			
ICED TEA			
SM	MED	LG	X-LG
$1⁶⁵	$1⁸⁰	$2⁰⁰	$2²⁰

MILK $.99
HOT COCOA *8oz* $1⁸⁰
COFFEE $1³⁵

IN-N-OUT BURGER

OPEN 10:30 a.m. to 1:00 a.m.
.................Fri. and Sat. until 1:30 a.m.

美式漢堡連鎖業者 In-N-Out Burger 的得來速菜單，照片年代日期不明

創新菜色

許多好點子的核心在於便利，本節著眼於創新，探討從冷凍食品到世界上最著名雞尾酒的許多事物。談到飲食，創造力的展現似乎不僅限於擺在您面前的盤子或玻璃杯中。

薩赫飯店的著名糕點盛放在它的招牌木盒裡

1832

世上最有名的巧克力蛋糕

薩赫蛋糕

·

香料圓環蛋糕

·

維也納蘋果捲

這種帶有杏桃果醬的濃厚巧克力蛋糕可能是奧地利最知名的產品之一，但與普遍看法相反，它在菜單上的出現宛如一場緩慢又穩定的賽跑。

提到薩赫蛋糕（Sachertorte）通常就會聯想到與它同名的維也納豪華旅館薩赫飯店（Hotel Sacher），而它的誕生絕大部分該歸功於廚師愛德華·薩赫（Eduard Sacher），然而第一代薩赫蛋糕其實是愛德華的父親弗朗茲·薩赫（Franz Sacher）製作的。

一八三二年，十六歲的弗朗茲在梅特涅親王（Prince Wenzel von Metternich）的廚房裡當學徒，有一次主廚在重要的晚宴當晚病倒了，弗朗茲臨時趕製這款蛋糕，結果眾人讚不絕口，成了烹飪史上影響深遠的大作。不過，得等到弗朗茲的兒子愛德華成為糕點師傅，再度採用父親的食譜，並於一八七六年將它列入薩赫飯店的菜單，薩赫蛋糕才真正引起了轟動。

薩赫蛋糕的食譜向來完全照舊且祕不外傳，直到愛德華的孫子小弗朗茲將食譜賣給了德梅爾糕點鋪（Demel）並導致冗長的訴訟糾紛。裁決結果？只有薩赫飯店可以聲稱擁有原始食譜，德梅爾不得對「原始的愛德華·薩赫蛋糕」有異議。兩種配方的主要區別在於，薩赫版的果醬位於兩層巧克力海綿蛋糕之間，德梅爾版的果醬則位於海綿蛋糕頂部但被巧克力淋面所覆蓋。

如今，每年大約有三十六萬個薩赫蛋糕被吃掉，每個蛋糕都有巧克力印章飾樣並搭配鮮奶油。但飯店菜單上的原創點心不單單只有它而已。薩赫蛋糕洋洋得意的身影旁邊，還有已經供應了一百八十多年的香料圓環蛋糕（spiced Bundt cake）和維也納蘋果捲（Viennese apple strudel）。

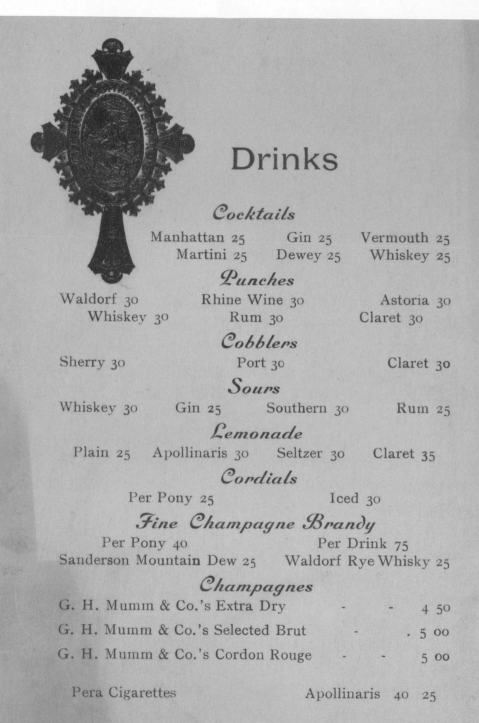

Drinks

Cocktails

Manhattan 25   Gin 25   Vermouth 25
Martini 25   Dewey 25   Whiskey 25

Punches

Waldorf 30   Rhine Wine 30   Astoria 30
Whiskey 30   Rum 30   Claret 30

Cobblers

Sherry 30   Port 30   Claret 30

Sours

Whiskey 30   Gin 25   Southern 30   Rum 25

Lemonade

Plain 25   Apollinaris 30   Seltzer 30   Claret 35

Cordials

Per Pony 25   Iced 30

Fine Champagne Brandy

Per Pony 40   Per Drink 75
Sanderson Mountain Dew 25   Waldorf Rye Whisky 25

Champagnes

G. H. Mumm & Co.'s Extra Dry   - -   4 50

G. H. Mumm & Co.'s Selected Brut   -   . 5 00

G. H. Mumm & Co.'s Cordon Rouge   - -   5 00

Pera Cigarettes   Apollinaris 40 25

The Waldorf-Astoria   January 23, 1914.

一九一四年，美國華爾道夫－阿斯托里亞飯店的飲品單

馬丁尼初體驗

不好意思，這種雞尾酒雖稱經典，而且看起來挺單純，它的歷史卻實在難以說清楚。

儘管眾說紛紜，但是至少可以肯定地說這是美國的發明，最有可能出現在十九世紀末。不過究竟是來自加州舊金山的酒吧，還是紐約的飯店，還有得吵。無論源於何處，自從這種飲料在湯馬斯（Jerry Thomas）一八八七年的著作《調酒師指南》（*Bartender's Guide*）中亮相之後，它的人氣就未曾稍減。

早期的馬丁尼調酒偏甜，通常是一半琴酒，一半苦艾酒，有時還帶有檸檬味。「乾」（dry）馬丁尼直到二十世紀初才開始流行。諷刺的是，此時正值禁酒年代，就在這段苦艾酒難以取得、只能以私釀酒做為主成分的時期，馬丁尼確立了其基本成分。這一點反過來又促成馬丁尼進軍歐洲，美國佬跑去開了美式酒吧，從此古典雞尾酒（old fashioned）、茱莉普酒（julep）和馬丁尼開始在全世界廣受歡迎。

從這份一九一四年華爾道夫－阿斯托里亞飯店（Waldorf-Astoria）的飲品單可看到，馬丁尼「最受歡迎酒類」的地位難以撼動，與之並列的曼哈頓調酒則是由威士忌、苦艾酒和苦精調和而成，據說發源於十九世紀末的紐約（嗯，不意外）。

一九二七年，《星期六晚間郵報》（Saturday Evening Post）的廣告

1901

為什麼吃豆子就找亨氏

鋪在烤吐司上、夾在帶皮的烤馬鈴薯中、擺在煎鍋內的雞蛋旁（但不碰到蛋）……焗豆已經等同於英國人童年時光的家庭慰藉。

有鑑於此，以下提到的事實可能令人驚訝。首先，焗豆是美國產品，最初是從大西洋彼岸進口過來的，直到美國亨氏食品公司在英國建立工廠之前，進口輸入持續了整整二十年。其次，亨氏焗豆最初被視為奢侈品，一九〇一年於倫敦的高級百貨公司 Fortnum & Mason 開始販售。

在維多利亞時代（1837-1901），英式早餐是用來向客人展示豪華富裕的方式之一，但到了英王愛德華時代（1901-1914），中產階級將英式早餐做為家庭正餐。很容易買到的焗豆和其他同樣容易取得的原料——培根、雞蛋、血腸——一起擺在盤子上，讓它的人氣穩定增長。

第二次世界大戰則使亨氏罐頭名聲大漲。雖然該品牌的番茄醬在戰爭期間由於糖短缺而從貨架上消失，但焗豆在政府食品部的倡導下被列為「必需品」，社會各階層都將它當作日常飲食。

在左頁這則一九二七年的美國廣告中，亨氏的獨特賣點是以手工烘烤豆子，意味著風味更加出色。其實這項產品直到二〇〇八年才被重新命名為「亨豆子」（Heinz Beanz）。亨氏公司表示，更名原因有二：首先是為了紀念一九六〇年代的經典廣告詞「吃豆子就找亨氏」（Beanz Meanz Heinz），其次是因為完整的名稱念起來有點拗口。

THE PUCK PRESS

THE UNITED ST

AMERICAN AMBASSADOR *(who has to live on his salary)*.— Let me help y

一八〇六年,《頑童》雜誌(*Puck*)上的插畫,美國大使正在分菜,
向來自世界各國的達官顯貴呈送焗豆

TATES ABROAD.

ou to some more baked beans, Princess. My wife cooked them herself.

美國加州帕薩迪納市（Pasedena）的 In-N-Out Burger

得來速餐飲

漢堡／起司漢堡
·
薯條炸物／沙士

　　通俗地說，一般稱為「得來速」的免下車餐廳誕生在美國似乎合情合理。在一九四〇年代末和一九五〇年代初，汽車產業蓬勃發展，愈來愈多已婚女性從事全職工作，因此備餐及家庭時間變得更加注重速度和便利性。通過點餐窗口購買食物，省去下車麻煩，節省了寶貴的時間——就這樣，一種生活方式由此而生。

　　據報導，一九四七年，第一個得來速服務在極具象徵意義的六十六號公路（Route 66）*旁、密蘇里州春田市（Springfield）的紅巨人漢保店（Red's Giant Hamburg）開張。儘管最初只是個加油站，老闆錢尼（Red Chaney）還是決定擴展經營，販售漢堡。這樣做很剛好，因為他自己養的牛群便能提供漢堡肉原料。店名之所以這樣取，是因為招牌的尺寸小了些，「漢堡」（hamburger）就變成了「漢保」（hamburg）。

　　可想而知，熱潮不斷延燒，總部位於加州的 In-N-Out Burger 於一九四八年就打著「得來速」餐廳的名號開業。開業當天的菜單很簡單：漢堡、起司漢堡、薯條炸物和各種汽水。大約七十年後，儘管總有都市傳說言之鑿鑿，說美國西岸的三百三十四家 In-N-Out Burger 各有隱藏版菜單，菜單內容其實並沒有太大的擴增。這項創新當時趕上了加州高速公路網的發展，沒多久便出現了數十家同類餐館。

＊從芝加哥到洛杉磯，全長 3,945 公里，又稱為美國大街（Main Street of America）、母親之路（Mother Road）或威爾‧羅傑斯高速公路（Will Rogers Highway），在美國國力急速發展的年代扮演重要角色，可說是見證美國經濟起飛與歷史演進的道路之一。

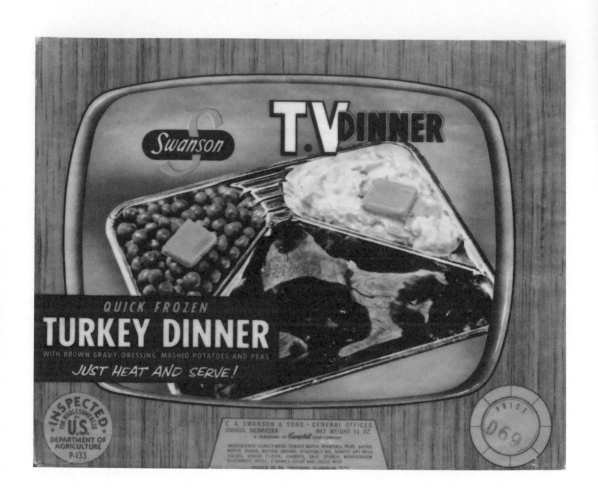

一九五四年，史雲生加熱火雞快餐的包裝盒，外型設計彷若電視機

1953

電視懶人快餐

火雞淋肉汁

·

馬鈴薯泥

·

青豆

　　電視節目這種美國國民娛樂消遣與富裕雙薪家庭的興起，無疑為「電視懶人」快餐（'TV' dinner，英國稱作「即食調理包」〔ready meal〕）的發明鋪陳了最好的局面。

　　說來有點好笑，第一道電視懶人快餐通常被認為與圍桌聚餐的感恩節有關。故事是這樣的，一九五三年，美國的史雲生父子食品公司（Swanson & Sons）正為了處理過剩火雞肉想方設法，當時一名員工無意間留意到了航空公司試著在長途航班內呈送熱食時使用的分格托盤。以此為出發點，製作出由火雞、肉汁、青豆、馬鈴薯泥和蔓越莓醬製成的晚餐組合，搭配使用的包裝盒外型仿照電視螢幕，甚至還有轉盤可以「調音量」。

　　電視懶人餐的到來宛如便利的王道福音，被職業婦女視為無須守著爐子數小時即可張羅好全家餐點的良方，該產品的首批廣告詞中有這麼一句：「遲到的是我，但不會是晚餐。」（I'm late–but dinner won't be.）

　　也許令人驚訝的是，這股風潮花了二十年左右的時間才跨越大西洋，而此與冰箱是大海彼岸較晚出現的奢侈品有關。英國人偏好的「即食調理包」──冷藏而非冷凍──一開始是一九七九年由 M&S（Marks & Spencer）推出的基輔雞，接著是一九八五年的中式和印度方便快餐。

名為「雞汁拉麵」的速食麵

1958

速食麵

　　速食麵餵養著全球的街坊小吃店和超市，它們成為速食商品對世界所造成的衝擊不亞於美國的電視懶人加熱快餐和英國的預製包裝三明治。

　　第一批以旺火快速微炸的乾麵是日籍臺裔發明家安藤百福研發的，由他所創辦的公司日清販售，一個個獨立包裝裡是內含雞肉調味料的一人份乾燥麵塊，品名為「雞汁拉麵」（Chikin Ramen）。這種乾麵條的價格比當時商店賣的新鮮麵條還貴，起初屬於奢侈品，但很快便超越了比它早上市行銷的麵條，成為最受歡迎的商品。

　　一九七〇年代，杯麵——塑膠容器內裝有乾麵塊並撒了調味料——問世，現在全世界每年消耗約一千億份速食麵。與其他速食食品不同，速食麵的本質並未因為多年來的技術發展而改變；不到五分鐘即可沖泡完成，享受麵食。

　　根據一項在日本進行的民意調查，日本民眾將速食麵的發明列為該國二十一世紀最偉大的成就之一。

上班日午餐必備

1980

超市三明治

蛋與水芹
·
鮭魚與番茄
·
美乃滋拌蝦子

有些食物的創新發明之所以具有革命性意義，箇中原因有對也有錯，預先製作並包裝好的三明治就是其中一種。

根據最近的市場調查，居住在英國的一般人每個月通常會吃掉二十個三明治，但在一九八〇年之前，三明治向來只是家庭廚房、酒吧或咖啡館才會出現的東西，你不會在超市、火車站或藥妝店看到它。

一九八〇年，M&S 在全英國五家分店推出了這項產品試水溫，與當今顯然豐富許多的餡料相比，當時菜單上的產品非常陽春：雞蛋配水芹、鮭魚佐番茄、美乃滋拌蝦子。有趣的是，儘管時代變了，某些事情仍然保持原貌：這些三明治今天依然在 M&S 銷售，最暢銷的仍舊是美乃滋拌蝦子。

三明治從家中臨時拼湊的餐點演變成平日午餐菜色的常客，無疑是工作環境壓力上升所促成的結果。隨著百貨公司開設三明治專賣櫃檯，同一棟建築中的咖啡餐館紛紛關上大門。一九八五年，Boots 成為第一家為三明治設立標準規格並在全國通路銷售包裝三明治的公司，也讓在餐館享用熱呼呼的午餐隨之成為歷史畫面。

維多利亞時期的銅板價冰品小販向殷殷期盼的群眾賣冰淇淋

1932

英國的冰淇淋小史

香草

·

什錦水果

·

巧克力脆片

·

蘭姆酒漬葡萄

　　數百年來，繽紛多姿的冰淇淋在全世界廣受歡迎。據說冰淇淋是一千多年前的中國人發明的，十三世紀時由馬可·波羅（Marco Polo）傳回義大利。由於缺乏有效的冷凍技術，等到十九世紀後期才在英國普及。在此之前，取得冰塊是一件大事，吃一碗冰淇淋是歐洲上層階級的專屬特權。

　　儘管其口號「停一下，買一個」（'Stop Me and Buy One'）已經成為英國經典廣告詞，但沃爾（Wall's）這個以冰淇淋（還有，呃，香腸）聞名的英國老品牌並不是騎三輪車賣冰淇淋的先驅。這種做法至少可追溯到一九○七年，當時從義大利南部搬到蘇格蘭的莫雷利（Giuseppe Morelli）與小兒子以騎三輪車的方式在當地開始叫賣冰淇淋。一九三二年，這位義式冰淇淋商人搬到富裕的海濱小鎮，肯特郡的布羅德斯泰爾（Broadstairs），進而創立了如今英國歷史最悠久的冰淇淋店之一。店內有氣泡水機、自動點唱機、用皮革包覆的座位，並提供八種口味的冰淇淋，外加彩寶聖代（knickerbocker glory）──英國海濱遊客的專屬享受。當時最受歡迎的口味包括香草、什錦水果（tutti frutti）、巧克力脆片以及（有些人或許會有不同意見的）蘭姆酒漬葡萄乾。

DELMONICO'S · FOUNDED 1827

Blue Point oysters 30 Cocktail 35		Cherrystone clams 35 Cocktail 40
Cotuits 35 Cocktail 40		Little Neck clams 30 Cocktail 35
Buzzard Bays 35 Cocktail 40		

HORS D'ŒUVRES

Sardines 50　　Anchovies 50　　Smoked salmon 50　　Queen olives 30　　Ripe olives 35
Stuffed olives 35　　Crab flake cocktail 65　　Garden celery 30　　Lobster cocktail 80

SOUPS

Purée of lentils 40
Cup, Hanan 60　　Purée split pea 40　　Oyster stew 55　　Green turtle 60　(15 minutes)
Clam broth 35　　Tomato 40　　Chicken okra 45　　Mongol 40　　Julienne 40
COLD IN CUP:　　Consommé 35　　Strained gumbo 45　　Chicken broth 40

EGGS

Ready　　　　　　　　　　　　　　*To Order*
Poached, Benedict 45　　　　　Shirred à la Turque (2) 65

FISH

Ready　　　　　　　　　　　　　　*To Order*
Live cod, Dutch style 75　　　　　　Bluefish, Meunière 75
Fried smelts, Remoulade sauce 75　　Striped bass, Maitre d'Hôtel 70
Stuffed crabs 65　　　　　　　　　Scallops and shrimps, Marinière 80

Plats du Jour　　　　　　　　　　Entrees

Ready　　　　　　　　　　　　　　*To Order*
Boiled fowl and rice, celery sauce 1 00　　Lamb chop, Robinson 75
Leg of lamb, parsnips in cream 85　　　　Veal kidney saute, Robert 90
Wiener schnitzel, noodles 80　　　　　　Half Guinea chicken broiled, bacon 1 50
Baked pork and beans 75　　　　　　　　Fresh mushrooms on toast 80

ROASTS　　　　　　　　　　　　GRILL

Ready　　　　　　　Chicken (half) 1 30　(whole) 2 50
Lamb 80　　Ribs of beef 90　　Lamb chops 95　　Mutton chop 75

VEGETABLES

Noodles 30　　　　　　　　　　Brussels sprouts 40
Oyster Bay asparagus 65　　New string beans 45　Cauliflower in cream 45　French peas 50
Spinach 40　Macaroni 35　Spaghetti 35　New beets in butter 35　Fried egg-plant 30
POTATOES: Boiled new 25　　Baked (1) 20　　Mashed 25　　Sautées 30　　Fried 25
Hashed in cream 30　　　　　　Seybel or Julienne 30　　　　Lyonnaise 35
Hashed in cream, gratinées 35　　Sweet potato 25　　Hashed browned 30

COLD BUFFET

Lobster, Mayonnaise (half) 1 00　　Lobster salad 1 25　　　　Virginia ham 80
Chicken salad 1 00　　Crabmeat salad 75　　Shrimp salad 75　　Beef salad 65
Sliced chicken 90　Smoked ham 65　Lamb 80　Roastbeef 90　Corned beef 65
Beef tongue 75　　　　　Assorted meats 1 00　and chicken 1 25

SALADS

Tomato and green pepper 45　Watercress 30　Potato 30　Chiffonade 50　Cucumber 35
Macédoine 50　　Beets 35　　String beans 45　Lettuce 35　Tomato 35　Romaine 35
Mayonnaise dressing 10 cents extra.

DESSERT

Compot of fresh fruit 45　　Plain rice pudding 30　Apple sauce 20　Stewed prunes 30
Vanilla, coffee or chocolate éclairs 20　　Rum cake 25　　　　Pie 20
Caramel custard 30　　　Charlotte Russe 30　　Bar-le-Duc jelly 40
Baked apple 20　with cream 30　　Fresh fruit tart 25　Cup custard, vanilla or chocolate 25
FRUITS.　　　Grape fruit, (half) 35　　Pineapple 25　　　　Orange 20
Pear 20　　　　Banana 15　　　Apple 20
FRENCH ICE CREAMS:　　Coffee 35　　　Vanilla 35　　　Chocolate 35
CHEESE: Gruyère 30 Port-du-Salut 30 Roquefort 50 Gervais 25 American 25 Liederkranz 30
Coffee with milk, pot p. p. 25 for two 35　　Tea, pot, p. p. 25 for two 35
"　"　cream　"　35　"　45　　Kaffee Hag, demie tasse 20
Kaffee Hag, pot, with cream 40
Horlick's malted milk 10

Beaver & South William Streets.　　　　　　　Tuesday, October 23, 1917

紐約傳奇餐館「戴爾莫尼克」的菜單

經典菜單

有人帶頭起而行，就會有其他人追隨，談到具有開創性的飲食趨勢時，尤其如此。以下幾頁將對餐飲業偶像級餐館、開拓者和文化機構的菜單致敬，涵蓋了精緻的奢華餐宴、具有道德意識的飲食方式等。

1893

引領潮流的戴爾莫尼克餐館菜單

蘭霍夫在烹飪方面的專業幾乎無與倫比。他十二歲時被送往巴黎學習糕點製作，一八六二年二十六歲時才回到紐約，開始在戴爾莫尼克餐館（Delmonico's）掌廚。

戴爾莫尼克餐館在過去幾世紀已逐漸成為典範的化身。身為美國最奢華的餐廳之一，據傳好幾道如今的美國經典佳餚都發源於此，諸如火焰霜淇淋（baked Alaska）、紐伯格龍蝦（Lobster Newberg）、瓣沙拉（wedge salad），以及在蘭霍夫時代就是經典的厚切牛排，通常稱為戴爾莫尼克牛排（Delmonico-style steak）。

然而，這些菜餚背後的許多故事現在聽起來宛如神話，不像是真實事件，紐伯格龍蝦就是個很好的例子。據說，知名船長溫伯格（Ben

紐約戴爾莫尼克餐館的外觀，照片年代日期不明

Wenberg）將這道菜介紹給餐廳老闆戴爾莫尼克（Lorenzo Delmonico），戴
爾莫尼克品嘗後便堅持將這道菜放進菜單。經過大廚蘭霍夫為它妝點增色並
做了細微改良後，這道菜一推出就獲得熱烈迴響。但為什麼叫做紐伯格呢？
這道菜最初以船長溫伯格的名字命名，由於發生了些爭執，就將船長名字的
字母易位重排後定為名稱。紐伯格龍蝦如此受歡迎，甚至連法國食譜和菜單
中也開始出現這道菜的蹤影，相當不簡單。

　　六十四頁這份極具蘭霍夫風格的菜單來自一八九三年一名警長的晚宴：
經典的法式烹調方式，以及完完全全的美式食材，包括馬里蘭州的甲魚類水
產、美國牛肉淋熟成肋眼醬汁（蘭霍夫菜單中的必備菜）、北美灰背野鴨佐
玉米糊，最後是「花式冰淇淋」。

First Panel
Sheriff's Jury
Annual Dinner

Wednesday, January 18th, 1893

Delmonico's

MENU

Oysters

SOUPS

Bisque of Crabs   Green Turtle, clear

SIDE DISH

Timbales, Reynière

FISH

Fillet of Bass, Joinville
Potatoes, Dauphine

REMOVE

Chablis   Fillet of Beef with Madeira
Sherry   Tomatoes, Trevise

Liebfraumilch   **ENTRÉES**
Chât. Lagrange   Breast of Chicken, Genin
Champagne   Peas, Parisian fashion

Macon Vieux   Terrapin, Maryland
Liqueurs
Apollinaris   SHERBET, PRUNELLE

ROAST

Canvas-back Ducks   (Fried Hominy)

COLD

Terrine of foies gras with Jelly
Lettuce Salad

SWEET

Pears, Ferrières

Pyramids

Fancy Ice Creams   Fruits   Cakes
Coffee

一八九三年，戴爾莫尼克餐館的菜單

蘭霍夫著作《美食家》的扉頁，一八九四年出版

Diner du 26 Juin 1900

MENU

Melon

Consommé Rossini

Crème Princesse

Truite Saumonée Norvégienne

Suprèmes de Volaille aux Artichauts

Selle de Pré-Salé à la broche

Petits Pois Française

Pommes nouvelles

Sorbets au Kirsch

Caneton de Rouen Vendôme

Cœurs de Romaine

Asperges Sauce Mousseline

Biscuit glacé Viennois

Friandises

Corbeilles de Fruits

VINS

Xérès   Pommery 1893 sec et doux

Château Caillou 1888   Grand vin

Château Smith Lafitte 1878   Château Giscours 1874

HOTEL RITZ   PARIS

一九〇〇年，巴黎麗緻飯店的菜單

1900

麗緻酒店的艾斯科菲耶

　　艾斯科菲耶（Auguste Escoffier）無疑是歐洲烹飪史上最重要的人物之一。他創造的烹調手法將承襲自師父卡漢姆（Marie-Antoine Carême）的精緻奢華烹飪風格變得流暢又優雅，今日已被視為經典法國廚藝的源頭。

　　艾斯科菲耶最著名的成就之一是編寫了至今仍被廣泛做為參考資料的《烹飪指南》（*Le Guide Culinaire*），並在書中將五種基本底醬確立為法國美食的骨幹。除了這些成就，艾斯科菲耶還在好幾間地位崇高的歐洲大飯店擔任廚師，好比倫敦的薩沃伊飯店（The Savoy）與後來的巴黎麗緻酒店（The Ritz）。

　　艾斯科菲耶原本受僱於里茲（Caesar Ritz），在南法管理蒙地卡羅大飯店（The Grand Hotel in Monte Carlo），直到一八九〇年才前往倫敦薩沃伊飯店。他和里茲——這位經理與他一起去了倫敦——在薩沃伊飯店服務的八年中，從威爾斯親王到法國演員莎拉·伯恩哈特（Sarah Bernhardt）等上流社會人士都受到吸引，成為座上賓。

　　大約五年後，艾斯科菲耶和里茲因涉嫌欺詐被解僱，兩個人便跑到巴黎創立了麗緻酒店，由此開始，原本不幸的際遇反倒促成了一家老字號的大飯店。

　　左頁這份菜單來自麗緻酒店，內容包含了許多人人皆識得的菜餚，幾乎可等同於二十一世紀典型法國小酒館的菜單：清燉肉湯、雞胸肉佐朝鮮薊、讓口氣清新的櫻桃冰沙，以及做為甜點的法式杏仁蛋糕和水果。

Supper

Malpecques 40   Cape Cods 30   Bluepoints 30   Cotuits 30

Bieluga Caviare 1 50   Pim-Olas 35   Lyon Sausage 50
Sardines 35   Carciofini 40   Antipasti 40
Radishes 25   Pickled Lamb's Tongue 40   Anchovies 50

HOT

Chicken Broth per cup 30   Chicken Broth, Bellevue per cup 30
Consommé cup 25   Clam Broth cup 25

Terrapin 3 50   Oyster Crabs 1 00
Stuffed Lobster 60   Crab Meat, Astoria 1 00
Lobster Cutlets, Cream sauce 60   Lobster, Bordelaise 1 25
Stuffed Crab 50   Broiled Lobster 1 00   Devilled Kidneys 50
Bouchée, Capucin 1 00   Chicken à la King 1 50
Canapé Waldorf 60   Sweetbreads, Waldorf 1 25
Boneless Hamburg Chicken 1 50   Lamb Chops, St. Hilaire 85
Scotch Woodcock 50   Welsh Rarebit 40   Yorkshire Buck 60

Broiled Chicken 2 00 half 1 00   Broiled Squab 90   Broiled Sweetbread 1 00
Tournedos of Filet, Cherron 1 50

Partridge 2 50   Mallard Duck 2 00   Woodcock 2 50

French Asparagus 1 25   German Asparagus 1 00
Artichoke, Hollandaise 60   Oyster Bay Asparagus 75

COLD

Partridge 2 50   Plover 90
Game Pie 1 25   Spring Lamb 80   Crabs, Ravigotte 60
Mixed Cold Meat 75 with Chicken 1 00   Fantaisie, Joseph 1 25
Beef à la Mode 75 Boneless Squab in jelly 1 10   Boned Capon 1 00
Westphalian Ham 75   Squab 90   Virginia Ham 75

Sandwiches:—Tongue 25   Chicken 30   Caviare 40
Sardine 30   Paté de foie gras 50   Club 35
Canapé à la Rex 50   Ham 25

Crab 75   Romaine 50   Alexander 75   Russian 1 00   Cucumbers 50
Lettuce 50   Chicken 1 00   Florida 75   Lobster 1 00
Tomato 50   Dixie 60   Japonaise 1 00

Nesselrode Pudding 40   Mixed Cakes 25   Sorbet au Curaçao 30
Café Parfait 25   Chestnut Plombière 40   Biscuit glacé 30
Charlotte Russe 25   Eclairs 25
Caramel Custard 30   Coupe St. Jacques 60

ICES IN SOUVENIRS 75

Peach Ice Cream 25   Peach frappée 25
Vanilla, Strawberry, Pistache, Coffee or Chocolate Ice Cream 25   Mixed 30
Apricot, Raspberry, Lemon, Orange or Pineapple Water Ice 25
French Coffee, Cup 15   Turkish Coffee 20
APOLLINARIS 40 20   **JOHANNIS 40 20**   10-11-05

11. Oct. 1905

一九〇五年，華爾道夫－阿斯托里亞飯店的菜單

1897

紐約最知名飯店的晚餐

魚子醬開胃小菜
·
燒烤牛肉
·
華爾道夫沙拉

　　紐約市中心曼哈頓的華爾道夫－阿斯托里亞飯店（Waldorf-Astoria）可稱得上是全世界最著名的旅館。最初是兩家各自獨立的飯店：位於馬路一側的華爾道夫飯店（Waldorf）於一八九三年開業，另一側則是建於一八九七年的阿斯托里亞飯店（Astoria）。第一家飯店的擁有者是上流社會知名的阿斯特家族（the Astor family），並以他們的德國故鄉命名，第二家飯店的取名緣由，想想他們的姓氏就明白了。

　　開幕之初，蓋飯店這個點子被當成了笑柄；當地人認為這在如此富裕的地區完全是畫蛇添足，而且對於那些進城出差的人來說，這樣的住宿太昂貴了，飯店的初始目的規劃不明。然而，舉辦了一連串募款晚宴之後，這間飯店受到上流社會人士的喜愛，聲譽從此鞏固不搖，來自世界各地的富人蜂擁而至，成為當時最大、最豪華的飯店。

　　華爾道夫－阿斯托里亞飯店是世界上第一家提供客房服務的飯店，人人都認得的流行菜餚也是由它促成的，好比由蘋果、芹菜、葡萄和核桃製成，與飯店同名的華爾道夫沙拉（Waldorf Salad）；好比班尼迪克蛋（儘管是否為初次供應此菜之處尚有爭議）與千島醬。

　　左頁這份一九〇五年的菜單可讓人感受到華爾道夫－阿斯托里亞飯店散發的奢華：一‧二五美元的野味餡餅和五十美分的鵝肝醬，在當時絕對是一筆不小的開銷，但從它總有常客光臨這點看來，應該不是沒理由的。

THE TOWER
Café Restaurant

The Most Beautiful Dining Room out of London.

EVERYTHING OF THE BEST
AT REASONABLE PRICES.

FOUR BILLIARD TABLES
(By Borroughes & Watts)

ADMISSION FREE

From Promenade and Bank Hey Street.

一九〇五年七月，黑潭塔節目單上的廣告

1905

去黑潭塔宴會廳吃頓飯、跳支舞

羊排

·

臀肉牛排

·

格羅夫斯和惠特納爾釀酒廠的艾爾啤酒和司陶特啤酒

黑潭（Blackpool）是英國各種社會階級都極愛的海濱旅遊勝地，而這與那座五百一十八英尺高的塔樓關係匪淺，該塔的外觀意圖模仿法國巴黎最有名的地標。

如今的黑潭塔（Blackpool Tower）已被公認是維多利亞式建築的典範，但在當時，它是蓬勃發展的沿海度假勝地又一創新之作。建築裡頭容納了一座水族館、一個充滿異國動物且有小丑常駐的馬戲團、一間舉辦各種表演和舞會的宴會廳，以及一間管弦樂隊會在樓中樓表演的音樂餐廳。塔樓和下面的紅磚建築群從頭到尾花了三年時間才建成，且根據一八九五年黑潭塔及其景點的導覽小冊子所述，在國定假日連著周末的連假期間會有多達五萬名遊客造訪。

黑潭塔的宴會廳擁有全英國最長的酒吧，酒吧裝飾著「精美的鏡子、華麗的彩繪鑲板和所有用具的完整展示牆……整合起來成為全英國的最佳展覽之一」。塔樓的餐廳同樣高雅，場地中央有一座餐廳專屬的「噴泉，有時候小巧玲瓏的噴嘴還會有電燈照明」。據說燒烤料理非常棒，羊排和臀肉牛排是每日常見的主要菜色，並搭配格羅夫斯和惠特納爾釀酒廠（Groves and Whitnall）的艾爾啤酒和司陶特啤酒。儘管黑潭塔及其相關設施漸漸不如以往風光，但仍保有文化意義。

Luncheon

Consomme Brunoise   Potage St. Germain

Supreme of Whitefish Vin Blanc
Salmon Fish Cakes Maryland

Scrambled Eggs with Truffles
Braised Ox Tail Printaniere
Macaroni al Sugo

Roast Loin of Pork and Dressing, Apple Sauce
Broccoli en Puree   Mashed Turnips
Baked Jacket and Fried Potatoes

Grilled Tenderloin Hamburger and Onions

COLD:
Roast Beef, Horseradish Sauce
Galantine of Veal   London Brawn   Pressed Beef
Roast Lamb, Mint Sauce

Salads—Romaine   Tomato
Mixed Pickles

Boiled Jam Roll Pudding, Cream Sauce

Ice Cream and Wafers

Cheese   Rolls

Tea   Coffee

———————

Passengers on Special Diet are invited to make known their
requirements to the Chief Third Class Steward

T/C

一九三七年，英國皇家郵政瑪麗皇后號的菜單

1937

橫渡大西洋時吃些啥

　　西歐和紐約市之間的跨大西洋之旅可能是有史以來最讓人充滿浪漫想像的航線之一。由於航程需花費六到七天，不難理解為什麼航程就和目的地本身一樣重要。

　　冠達－白星航運（Cunard-White Star Line）打造了好幾艘短命且可說是注定沒有未來的船隻，英國皇家郵政瑪麗皇后號（RMS Queen Mary）即其中之一，也是一九三〇年代裝飾最精美的航班輪船之一，從南安普敦（Southampton）開往瑟堡（Cherbourg），然後再到紐約。

　　依循當時的裝飾藝術風，瑪麗皇后號的裝潢既時尚又優雅，獲得「木料之船」美稱。據報導，家具和裝飾總共用了五十種不同的木頭。從邱吉爾（Winston Churchill）、艾略特（T. S. Eliot）、伊麗莎白・泰勒（Elizabeth Taylor）到華特・迪士尼（Walt Disney）等名人都曾是頭等艙乘客。

　　雖然左頁的菜單看起來像是為電影明星準備的，實際上是供應給三等艙乘客的餐點，而且是船上典型的每日午餐。這些菜餚反映了旅途中每個停靠港的當地口味，包括馬里蘭風格的蟹餅、漢堡、春季時蔬燉牛尾湯和非常有英式風味的烤牛肉佐辣根醬。

　　無論何種艙等，餐廳和供應的食物都是精心製作的，可是這些精巧並不長久，因為這艘船在第二次世界大戰期間被挪為部隊運輸之用，之後才重新回歸商業用途。一九六七年十月三十一日是瑪麗皇后號最後一次航行，啟航前往美國西海岸並抵達加州長灘後便永久停泊繫留。這艘輪船現在已成為旅遊勝地，並設有博物館、酒吧、餐廳和娛樂場所。

午餐菜單封面插圖

怪咖餐廳原版菜單中的插圖

1961

怪咖素食餐廳

英國家常蔬菜派

·

小扁豆沙拉

·

起司司康

　　儘管道德素食主義和天然食材有益健康的信念一九六〇年代前就已存在，但以蔬食為主的生活方式較被主流意識廣泛接受，仍然發生在這充滿變革的十年之間。

　　的確，早在維多利亞時代就有素食餐廳，比如位於伯明罕（Birmingham）的皮特曼素食飯店（Pitman Vegetarian Hotel）於一八九八年開業，以當時素食協會（Vegetarian Society）副主席的名字命名，一直營業到一九三〇年代。怪咖餐廳（Cranks）的創始人坎特（David Canter）則把握時機，在倫敦市內充滿活力的卡納比街（Carnaby Street）開設了一家天然食材沙拉吧，於一九六一年開始流行的自由主義時代氛圍中乘勢而起。

　　怪咖提供全麥麵包、蛋糕和鹹派，以及讓顧客吃到飽的自助式沙拉和起司。英國家常蔬菜派、小扁豆沙拉和起司司康通常是主要班底，也是這家餐廳的招牌特色。不過由於菜單品項取決於可取用的農產品，因此幾乎每天都在變化。

　　怪咖餐廳不久後便開始引領時尚。一九六一年，《閒談者》（Tatler）雜誌推薦了它，並特別讚賞其「獨特的室內陳設」──木桌、手工陶瓷、組合不協調的裝潢──從此讓怪咖累積了一群名人粉絲，其中包括保羅·麥卡尼（Paul McCartney）、琳達·麥卡尼（Linda McCartney）與戴安娜王妃。幾十年來，「怪咖」從一家沙拉吧變成了連鎖餐廳，最後一家分店則於二〇一六年關閉，令人惋惜。

NITRO POACHED APERITIFS

Vodka and Lime Sour, Gin and Tonic, Tequila and Grapefruit

RED CABBAGE GAZPACHO

Pommery Grain Mustard Ice Cream

JELLY OF QUAIL, CRAYFISH CREAM

Chicken Liver Parfait, Oak Moss and Truffle Toast

(Homage to Alain Chapel)

SNAIL PORRIDGE

Iberico Bellota Ham, Shaved Fennel

SCALLOP IN AMOND MILK

ROAST FOIE GRAS

Barberry, Confit Kombu and Crab Biscuit

MAD HATTER'S TEA PARTY

(c. 1892)

Mock Turtle Soup, Pocket Watch and Toast Sandwich

二〇一四年，肥鴨餐廳的菜單

1995

肥鴨餐廳的神經美食學

英國歷史上很少有一家餐廳，或說是一名廚師，能與肥鴨餐廳（The Fat Duck）及其主廚布魯門索（Heston Blumenthal）一樣受到關注。

這家餐廳以漢普郡（Hampshire）布瑞村（Bray）一家傳統老酒吧的舊址為基礎，於一九九五年開張，不但獲得米其林三星級的殊榮，還頂著「世界最佳餐廳」的稱號。

儘管以賣牛排和薯條（信不信由你）起家，肥鴨餐廳卻成為所謂的多重感官美食的代名詞，這種技術將諸如聲音之類的感覺融入了用餐體驗。該餐廳最著名的招牌菜之一，「海洋之聲」（Sound of the Sea）正可體現這點。用餐的客人吃著各式各樣的貝類和可食用的海藻，同時聽著海浪拍擊海岸岩石的聲音。

雖然腦神經與美味的關係並不是大眾用餐時的優先考量要素，但布魯門索對沉浸式飲食的研究幾乎就像針對藝術形式的探索，引起了全世界的關注和讚譽。正如廚師自己說的，食物「具有產生大量記憶和情感的能力」。

肥鴨的菜單上還有頗受議論的蝸牛粥、培根雞蛋冰淇淋，兩者同樣深具革命意義，訴求主觀感受且內含顛覆的力量。

MAINS
主餐

菜單不只反映飲食流行趨勢，也是更廣闊社會歷史背景的一部分，而且述說的故事不僅與特定情境有關，還會提及後來衍生的成果遺產。本章內容全數涉及「重大」事件，從一八九七年維多利亞女王六十周年紀念日和一九〇一年史上第一次諾貝爾獎晚宴，到紅十字會在第一次世界大戰期間的食堂供餐與一九四八年新成立的英國國民保健署所提供的醫院伙食──這些菜單的概念，或僅僅只因其出現，就具體而微地概括了當時的社會和政治變化。而當這些菜單反映了廣泛的文化脈絡，食譜裡的菜單則揭示了家庭內部發生的變化。《比頓夫人的家務寶典》中的菜單大量呈現了維多利亞時代的社會流動性，帕頓的第一本彩色食譜則為當今美麗又光亮的大部頭烹飪書開了先例。

《英國佬》雜誌（*Blighty*）聖誕節特刊封面

創造歷史的餐點

宴飲用餐往往與重大事件同步。無論是各國領袖聚會、總統就職典禮，還是慶祝政治上改革進步的菜單，共同點都是反映過去、現在和未來的食物。

維多利亞女王就任六十周年紀念宴會的餐桌座位分配

1897

維多利亞女王
就任六十周年紀念餐宴

　　維多利亞女王的就任六十周年紀念餐宴具有雙重意義。在二〇一五年伊麗莎白二世女王的任期超過她之前，維多利亞女王是英國歷史上任期最長的君主。慶祝宴會這天被宣布為大英帝國的節日，在所有的英國領土都生效——當時維多利亞女王統治的臣民約四億五千萬人。儘管女王在丈夫去世後那幾年聲望下降，但由於工業化和領土擴張，此時的經濟蓬勃發展，女王的聲望也隨之飆升。

　　周年紀念日是六月二十二日，女王公開露面了數次，並與英國自治領和印度各邦領導人一起在倫敦市內遊行。六月二十一日舉行了遊行前夕的正式晚宴，女王的親人和貴賓們接受款待，享用了明顯帶有法國特色的盛宴。餐宴中除了提供很多道正餐，還提供了自助餐，客人可以品嘗如蘇格蘭肉湯、雞肉飯和英式豌豆料理等佳餚。自助餐區的其他餐點還包括了一道被略略提及的「冷熱燒鳥」（hot and cold roast fowl）和番茄沙拉。

次頁：皇家與皇室慶典的菜單

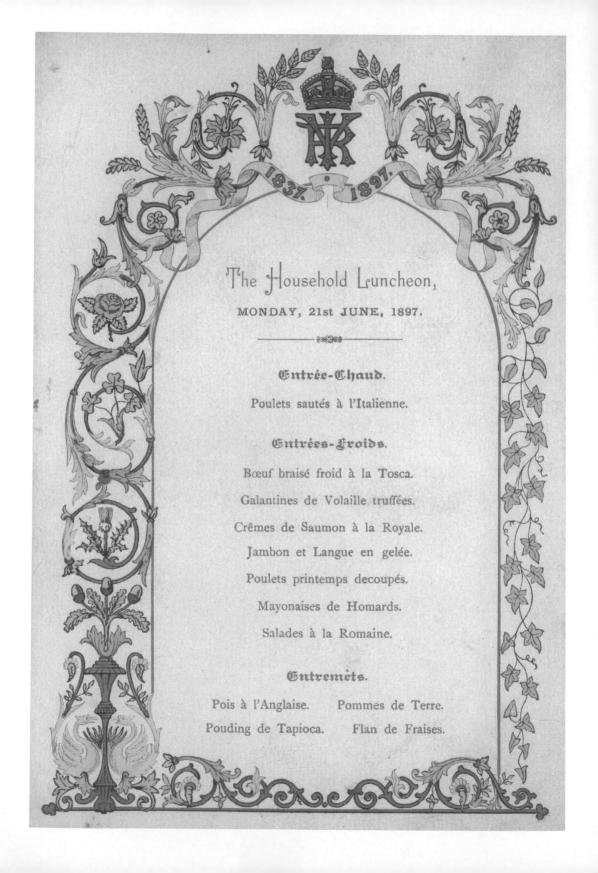

The Household Luncheon,

MONDAY, 21st JUNE, 1897.

Entrée-Chaud.

Poulets sautés à l'Italienne.

Entrées-Froids.

Bœuf braisé froid à la Tosca.

Galantines de Volaille truffées.

Crêmes de Saumon à la Royale.

Jambon et Langue en gelée.

Poulets printemps decoupés.

Mayonaises de Homards.

Salades à la Romaine.

Entremêts.

Pois à l'Anglaise.   Pommes de Terre.

Pouding de Tapioca.   Flan de Fraises.

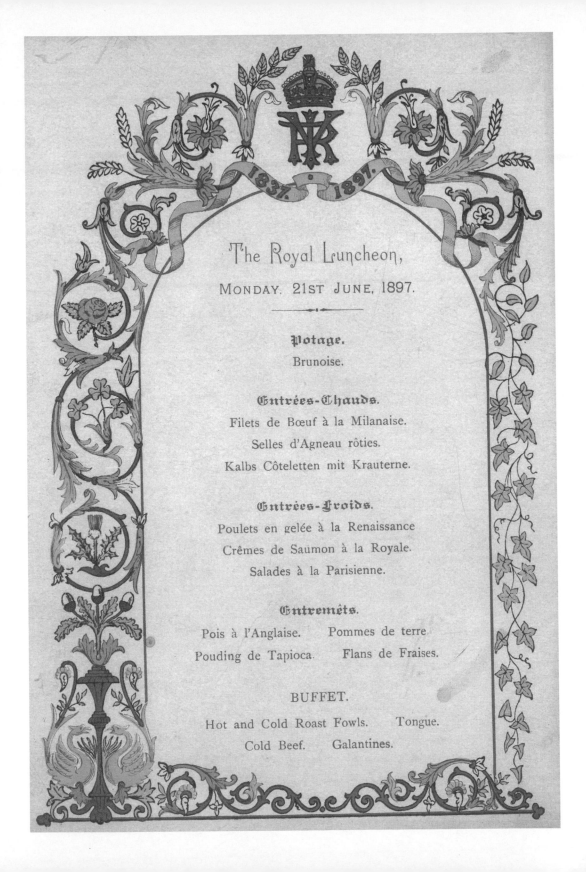

The Royal Luncheon,

MONDAY. 21ST JUNE, 1897.

Potage.

Brunoise.

Entrées-Chauds.

Filets de Bœuf à la Milanaise.

Selles d'Agneau rôties.

Kalbs Côteletten mit Krauterne.

Entrées-Froids.

Poulets en gelée à la Renaissance

Crêmes de Saumon à la Royale.

Salades à la Parisienne.

Entremêts.

Pois à l'Anglaise.   Pommes de terre

Pouding de Tapioca.   Flans de Fraises.

BUFFET.

Hot and Cold Roast Fowls.   Tongue.

Cold Beef.   Galantines.

首屆諾貝爾獎得主（從左上角起順時針）：杜南、倫琴、帕西、普魯東、馮·貝林、凡特荷夫

1901

第一屆諾貝爾獎晚宴

開胃菜／諾曼第醬煮鰈魚湯／菲力牛排
·
炙烤榛果松雞／成功大飯店的糕點

諾貝爾獎如今聲譽卓著，但起源其實有點複雜。這個獎項來自發明家阿爾弗雷德·諾貝爾（Alfred Nobel）的構想，他最為人熟知的發明是炸藥，該獎則是他眾多遺願中最後一項促成的。一八九六年，他去世的八年前，某法國報紙刊登了一則訃聞，誤認阿爾弗雷德已經過世，實際上死者是他兄弟工程師路維格·諾貝爾（Ludvig Nobel）。阿爾弗雷德的心神都被自己的遺產將被如何看待一事給盤據了，決定採取行動，將巨額財產留給一家基金會，該基金會每年將評判「帶給人類最大利益」的人，並頒發獎金。

第一次授獎儀式於一九〇一年十二月十日舉行，距他離世已有五年。物理、化學、醫學和文學這四項由斯德哥爾摩瑞典皇家音樂學院頒發，和平獎（可說是近代產生最多爭議的）典禮則在挪威奧斯陸舉行，當時這座城市仍叫克里斯蒂安那（Christiana）。第一屆獲獎者包括發現 X 光而獲得物理獎的倫琴（Wilhelm Conrad Röntgen）、因研究動植物體內的滲透壓而獲化學獎的凡特荷夫（Jacobus H. van't Hoff）、致力於尋找白喉療法而得到醫學獎的馮·貝林（Emil von Behring），普魯東（Sully Prudhomme）獲頒文學獎，國際紅十字會創始人杜南（Henry Dunant）與享譽國際的和平主義者帕西（Frédéric Passy）兩人則共同獲得和平獎。

典禮結束後，客人受邀到奧斯陸大飯店（The Grand Hotel, Oslo）參加慶祝晚宴。飯店餐廳供應經典法式菜餚，包括奶油醬煮鰈魚、菲力牛排和二十世紀初公認的美味佳餚榛果松雞。甜點則是從法國波爾多成功大飯店（Succès Grand Hôtel）遠道送來的高級糕點搭配香甜雪利酒。

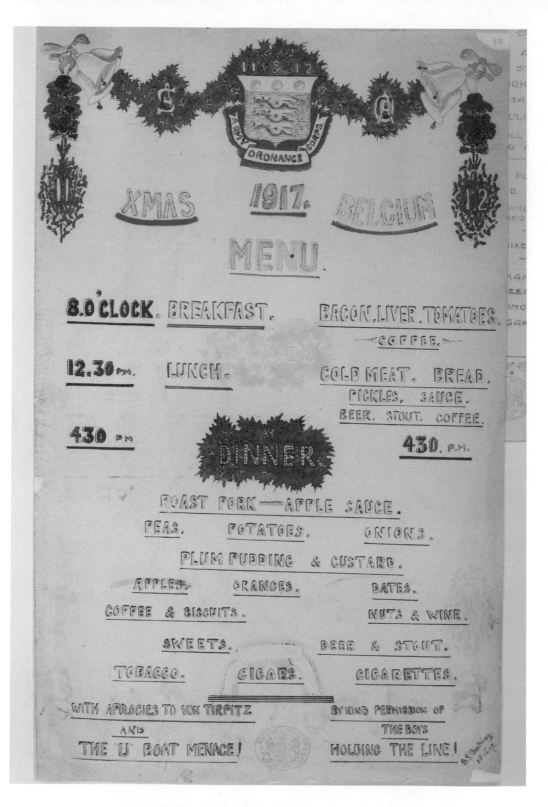

一九一七年，一份來自戰壕的聖誕節手寫菜單

1917

戰壕裡的聖誕節

　　關於一九一四年聖誕節休兵這件事已有不少人為文談過了，當時壕溝裡的部隊發起非正式停火，吟唱頌歌，交換口糧、菸酒，甚至一起踢足球。儘管這項活動很可惜僅有一次，不過在英國的人們仍繼續努力捎給為了一戰而服役的男性與女性同胞些許節日氣氛，印度和英國軍隊每年都會收到一包又一包糖果和香菸。一九一四年，陸軍總司令夫人發起一項活動，動員婦女一起為前線人員織圍巾，據報導最後總共發送了二十五萬條圍巾。

　　左頁是自一九一七年起便開始供應給比利時陸軍軍需部隊的伙食菜單。大後方的士兵還能享受相對優渥、近似聖誕大餐的飲食，前線士兵比較可憐，吃的仍然是平常配給的口糧，在可能的情況下才會收到額外的零食。諸如左頁裡的烤肉加蘋果醬、李子布丁、水果、堅果、糖果和香菸，都與一九一七年所有士兵的日常飯菜相去甚遠。無論駐紮在哪裡，部隊一般都是就地坐下來煮馬卡諾奇罐頭燉肉（Maconochie），罐頭內是較肥也較廉價的牛肉塊和馬鈴薯、胡蘿蔔、洋蔥，再搭配硬餅乾一起吃。

一九一七年，《戰爭畫報》（*The War Illustrated*）內一幅名為
〈頌歌與歡笑響徹戰壕〉（'Melody and Merriment Ringing in the Trenches'）的插圖

《倫敦新聞畫報》（*Illustrated London News*）中描繪的一九一四年聖誕節休兵

"Victory" Dinner,

FEBRUARY 22ND, 1918.

MENU.

Consommé Julienne.
ou
Crême de Volaille.

Turbot à la Mornay.
Pommes Nouvellee.

Lentil Cutlets and Tomato Sauce.
Eggs à l'Italienne.

Tarte de Rhubarbe.
Crême à la Vanilla.

Café.

一九一八年，婦女參政運動者的「勝利晚宴」菜單

1918

婦女參政運動者的勝利晚宴

　　打從一九一六年開張以來，倫敦霍爾本（Holborn）的密涅瓦咖啡館（Minerva Café）便是素食咖啡館和婦女參政運動、共產主義和無政府主義運動等各派人士的會面場所。這家咖啡館也是婦女自由聯盟（WFL, Women's Freedom League）的總部。當時一份發行並倡導婦女參政的報紙《票量》（The Vote）描述，密涅瓦咖啡館是「位於倫敦城區和西區或者說附近最棒、最誘人的地方，為您提供美味精緻的佳餚」，還特別指出「若有朋友願意資助，送他們舒適的椅子、一張切斯特菲爾德沙發和鋼琴，老闆們將由衷感謝」。

　　女性參政運動中常見素食主義者，許多人也反對穿皮草、吃肉和以動物做實驗。為了慶祝《人民代表法》（The Representation of the People Act）的通過（該法案給予婦女投票權），婦女自由聯盟舉辦了一九一八年二月的晚宴。這場「勝利晚宴」走魚素路線：鯪魚淋莫內起司醬（mornay sauce）、扁豆煎餅和大黃派。這家咖啡館甚至連使用的陶器也反映著經營者想傳達的激進理念「敢於自由」。

　　密涅瓦咖啡館最終發展成密涅瓦俱樂部，一個開放給所有政治主張強烈的男性和女性的機構。咖啡館則於一九五九年歇業，但保留了為最初成立它的女士們特地設計的匾額。

一九四三年，史達林、小羅斯福、邱吉爾於德黑蘭會議

1943

德黑蘭會議中的
史達林、邱吉爾與小羅斯福

波斯大麥湯

·

清燉鱒魚佐大白鱘魚子醬

·

烤火雞配烤馬鈴薯與季節時蔬

·

番紅花冰淇淋

·

起司舒芙蕾

　　在伊朗首都舉行的同盟國領袖會議標誌著對第二次世界大戰的看法發生了轉變。邱吉爾、小羅斯福和史達林首次聚在一起，同意在第二戰線上團結起來，進一步討論打敗納粹德國的計畫，並組建一個聯合組織以「消除這場為害了好幾代人的兵禍和恐懼」。

　　在蘇聯大使館舉行的會議為期四天，對談氣氛難免緊張激烈，由於會期第三天是邱吉爾生日，英國首相便決定在英國大使館內舉辦慶生晚宴。十一月三十日，邱吉爾為六十九歲生日晚宴精選了經典的英式菜餚，並加上幾道中東風味美食以向他們的所在地致意：首先以血腥瑪麗雞尾酒開場，接著是波斯大麥湯、清燉鱒魚佐魚子醬、烤火雞、番紅花冰淇淋，最後是起司舒芙蕾。這一餐的主角是一個用六十九支蠟燭排列成字母「V」以代表「勝利」的生日蛋糕，並由英國首相吹熄，史達林與小羅斯福分別坐在壽星兩側。

PEACE DINNER

given by

**THE FOREIGN PRESS
ASSOCIATION IN LONDON**

Guests of honour:
The Rt. Hon. Clement Attlee, Prime Minister

and

Delegates to the First
United Nations Assembly

In the Chair: Dr. H. W. EGLI
President of the Foreign Press Association

Thursday, February 7th, 1946 – 7.30 p.m.

SAVOY HOTEL

一九四六年，海外新聞協會舉辦的聯合國和平晚宴請帖封面

1946

聯合國和平晚宴

　　一九四五年，聯合國正式成立，最初由五十一個國家組成。各國代表聚集在加州舊金山起草了一部憲章，自此成為維護國際和平的藍圖。在第二次世界大戰造成的災難性後果之後，為了防止全球動盪再次發生，美國、英國、蘇聯和中國等所謂的四大同盟國早在一九四四年十月就舉行了會談，針對新國際組織的義務和限制達成協議。聯合國的細節、歷史和後續影響複雜微妙，短短幾句無法描述詳盡，這裡只需要知道第一屆聯合國大會（UN General Assembly）於一九四六年一月十七日在倫敦舉行。

　　三個星期後，海外新聞協會（FPA, Foreign Press Association）── 一個本身與政治沒有掛鉤的組織 ── 在倫敦舉辦了一項活動，以英國首相阿特利（Clement Atlee）為主要貴賓，聯合國代表和海外新聞協會的工作人員齊聚在薩沃伊飯店舉行了所謂的「和平晚宴」。

　　俏皮逗趣的「菜單」上畫著各國領導人的肖像漫畫，比如戴圓頂禮帽的鮭魚、長翅膀的山姆大叔，旨在諷刺各會員國，餐點如抗戰主菜（plat de resistance）、冷凍原子彈（bombe glacée atomique）和俄國波斯風的中國餐（chinoiseries Russo-Persanes）則提醒大家政治上的成見。這些料理是如何呈現的並沒有記載，但肯定幽默感十足。

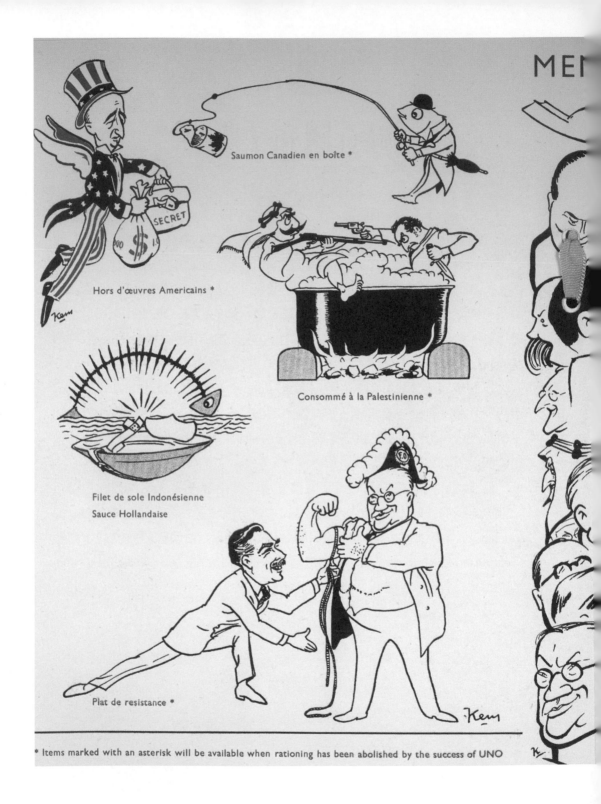

海外新聞協會晚宴菜單中的戲謔插畫

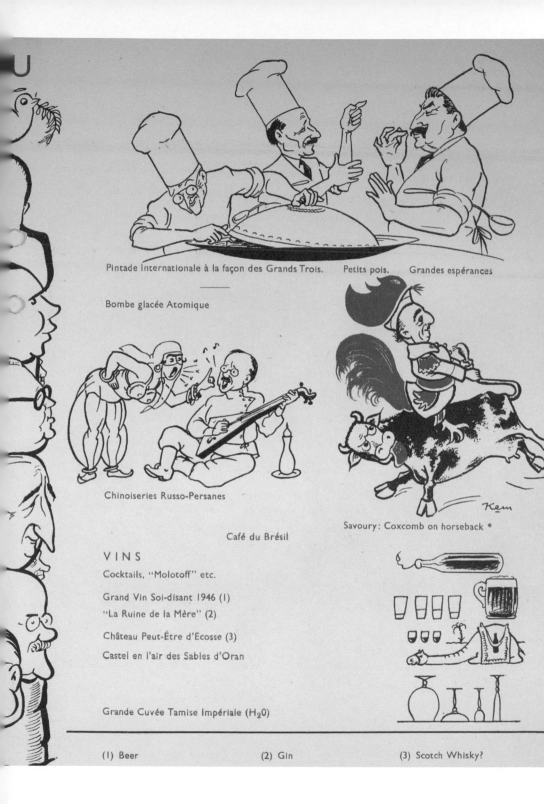

Pintade Internationale à la façon des Grands Trois.   Petits pois.   Grandes espérances

Bombe glacée Atomique

Chinoiseries Russo-Persanes

Savoury: Coxcomb on horseback *

Café du Brésil

VINS

Cocktails, "Molotoff" etc.

Grand Vin Soi-disant 1946 (1)

"La Ruine de la Mère" (2)

Château Peut-Être d'Ecosse (3)

Castel en l'air des Sables d'Oran

Grande Cuvée Tamise Impériale (H₂0)

(1) Beer   (2) Gin   (3) Scotch Whisky?

蒙巴頓勳爵在泰姬宮殿酒店的晚宴發表演說

1947

印度獨立紀念晚宴

香料調味的法式雞肉清湯
·
印度美食
·
雞肉舒芙蕾
·
水果和蛋白霜

經過漫長奮鬥，印度終於艱辛地脫離了英國，於一九四七年八月十五日午夜正式獨立。正當數百人聚集在孟買的印度門（Gateway of India）紀念建築旁，在泰姬宮殿酒店（Taj Palace Hotel）內，為了向印度獨立與巴基斯坦成為完全獨立的國家致敬，於擺脫殖民前夕舉行了晚宴。

這頓內含三道高級法國料理的晚餐以印度香料為基調，既反映了當時國家上層社會的風尚，也向愛國主義致敬。第一道菜是有香料調味的法式雞肉清湯，然後是「印度美食」雞肉舒芙蕾，最後是水果和蛋白霜餅（meringue，又譯馬林糖）。緊接在晚宴後還有演講、各種歌舞表演，最後是芭蕾舞演出。晚宴參加者皆為達官貴人，包括最後一任印度總督蒙巴頓勳爵（Lord Mountbatten）。隔天，整座城市充滿了慶祝活動，公共交通皆免費搭乘，方便人們在城市各處歡慶。

LUNCHEON

CAVIAR FRAPPE

CONSOMME, JULIENNE

OMELET WITH WALNUT JELLY, STRIP OF BACON

SHRIMPS CREOLE, WITH FLUFFY STEAMED RICE

FRIED YOUNG CHICKEN, WHITE WINE-FLAVORED, AU SEC

BAKED SUGAR-CURED HAM, CHAMPAGNE SAUCE

GARDEN PEAS   CREAM-WHIPPED POTATOES

SOUTHERN PACIFIC SALAD BOWL

CORN BREAD   HOT ROLLS

ICE CREAM, SWEET WAFERS

HOT APPLE PIE WITH CHEESE

ASSORTED CHEESE, TOASTED WAFERS

CHILLED CRANSHAW MELON

COFFEE   TEA   MILK

餐車上供應的食物

1959

赫魯雪夫在加州的鐵道晚宴

赫魯雪夫（Nikita S. Khrushchev）是史達林的接班人，也是蘇聯政權的忠實信徒。他就任蘇聯最高領導人期間，蘇聯與西方的關係既存在和平共存的日子，也曾面臨危機時刻。說到危機，總讓人想起一九六二年的古巴飛彈危機，和平共存最具代表性的事例則是赫魯雪夫前往美國進行國是訪問，也是蘇聯領導人第一次出訪美國。

一九五九年九月十五日，赫魯雪夫與妻子降落在美國土地上，受到美國總統艾森豪（Dwight David Eisenhower）的歡迎。副總統尼克森曾在訪問蘇聯和波蘭時鼓吹赫魯雪夫前往美國一遊，大概是溫情攻勢奏效，他便展開了為期兩星期的訪問，旅程中充滿認真的對談，包括連同加州在內的全美各地巡迴旅行。

左頁這份在洛杉磯和舊金山十三小時火車旅程內供赫魯雪夫夫婦挑選的菜單以英文和俄文寫成 —— 對俄國人的體貼禮遇最多就這樣了，供應的食物則完全是美式風格。早餐包括雞蛋、培根和新鮮桃子切薄片，午餐包括克里歐燴蝦（shrimps Creole）、炸雞、糖燻火腿淋香檳醬、南太平洋沙拉缽和熱蘋果派。伏特加酒被經典馬丁尼取而代之。

造訪好萊塢時，這位蘇聯最高領導人會見了瑪麗蓮‧夢露（Marilyn Monroe）、法蘭克‧辛納屈（Frank Sinatra）和伊麗莎白‧泰勒等大明星，但出於安全考量，取消了萬眾矚目的迪士尼樂園之旅。

LUNCHEON   ЗАВТРАК

CAVIAR, FRAPPE
ИКРА FRAPPE

CONSOMME, JULIENNE
БУЛЬОН JULIENNE

☐ OMELET WITH WALNUT JELLY, STRIP OF BACON
ОМЛЕТ С ВАРЕЬЕМ, БЭКОН

☐ SHRIMPS CREOLE, WITH FLUFFY STEAMED RICE
КРЕВЕТКИ CREOLE С РИСОМ НА ПАРУ

☐ FRIED YOUNG CHICKEN,
WHITE WINE-FLAVORED, AU SEC
ЖАРЕНЫЕ ЦЫПЛЯТА В БЕЛОМ ВИНЕ, AU SEC

☐ BAKED SUGAR-CURED HAM, CHAMPAGNE SAUCE
ЗАПЕЧЕННАЯ ВЕТЧИНА, СОУС CHAMPAGNE

GARDEN PEAS   CREAM-WHIPPED POTATOES
ЗЕЛЕНЫЙ ГОРОШЕК
КАРТОФЕЛЬНОЕ ПЮРЕ

SOUTHERN PACIFIC SALAD BOWL
САЛАТ SOUTHERN PACIFIC

CORN BREAD   HOT ROLLS
КУКУРУЗНЫЙ ХЛЕБ, ГОРЯЧИЕ БУЛОЧКИ

☐ ICE CREAM, SWEET WAFERS
МОРОЖЕНОЕ, БИСКВИТЫ

☐ HOT APPLE PIE WITH CHEESE
ЯБЛОЧНЫЙ ПИРОГ С ЛОМТИКАМИ СЫРА

☐ ASSORTED CHEESE, TOASTED WAFERS
ОТБОРНЫЕ СЫРЫ, ВАФЛИ

☐ CHILLED CRANSHAW MELON
ДЫНЯ CRANSHAW СО ЛЬДА

☐ COFFEE   ☐ TEA   ☐ MILK
КОФЕ,   ЧАЙ,   МОЛОКО

上圖：菜單隨附的點餐表單
次頁：赫魯雪夫夫婦跨越全美的鐵道之旅中提供的飲品單

НАПИТКИ   BEVERAGES

ВИСКИ, ДЖИН, КОНЬЯК и др.:	WHISKIES, GIN, BRANDIES, ETC.:

ШОТДАНДСКАЯ заграничная   *IMPORTED SCOTCH*

КАНАДСКАЯ с бандеролью   *CANADIAN, BONDED*

BOURBON OR RYE,
разлитая по бутылкам с бандеролью   *BOURBON OR RYE, BOTTLED IN BOND*

РОМ   *RUM*

ВОДКА   *VODKA*

ДЖИН домашнего производства   *GIN, DOMESTIC*

ВЫДЕРЖАННЫЙ КОНЬЯК
лучшего качества   *FINE OLD COGNAC BRANDY*

КАЛИФОРНИЙСКИЙ
КОНЬЯК   *CALIFORNIA GRAPE BRANDY*

КОКТЕЙЛИ: COCKTAILS:

MANHATTAN   *MANHATTAN*

DRY MARTINI   *DRY MARTINI*

VODKA MARTINI   *VODKA MARTINI*

OLD FASHIONED   *OLD FASHIONED*

ЛИКЕРЫ: LIQUEURS:

РАЗНЫЕ ЛИКЕРЫ   *VARIETY OF LIQUEURS*

ВИНА: WINES:

ХЕРЕС ИЛИ ПОРТВЕЙН   *SHERRY OR PORT*

ПИВО И ALE   BEER AND ALE

МИНЕРАЛЬНЫЕ ВОДЫ и др.:   MINERAL WATERS, ETC.:

SHASTA WATER   *SHASTA WATER*

CANADA DRY WATER   *CANADA DRY WATER*

GINGER ALE   *GINGER ALE*

ROOT BEER   *ROOT BEER*

COCA-COLA   *COCA-COLA*

PEPSI-COLA   *PEPSI-COLA*

DR. PEPPER   *DR. PEPPER*

7-UP   *7-UP*

PLUTO WATER   *PLUTO WATER*

CALSO WATER   *CALSO WATER*

WHITE ROCK WATER   *WHITE ROCK WATER*

ВИНОГРАДНЫЙ СОК   *GRAPE JUICE*

ОРАНЖАТ   *ORANGEADE*

ЛИМОНАД   *PLAIN LEMONADE*

POLAND WATER
«натуральная»   *POLAND WATER (NATURAL)*

INAUGURATION

LUNCHEON

JANUARY TWENTIETH

NINETEEN HUNDRED SIXTY-ONE

UNITED STATES SENATE RESTAURANT

UNITED STATES CAPITOL

1961

甘迺迪總統就職午宴

　　甘迺迪總統（John F. Kennedy）的就職前舞會由法蘭克·辛納屈主持，與會貴賓充滿了好萊塢熠熠星光，包括柯蒂斯（Tony Curtis）、貝拉方堤（Harry Belafonte）、羅斯科（Mark Rothko）、斯坦貝克（John Steinbeck）、海明威（Ernest Hemingway）和費茲傑羅（Ella Fitzgerald），很可能是美國首都有史以來最輝煌耀眼的派對之一。

　　這讓活動結束後在白宮舉行的午宴顯得相當平實家常。來自六個州的政治代表組成了午宴接待委員會，為午宴提供美國經典美食。這些佳餚表現了鄉村烹飪給人的溫馨撫慰感，又微妙地略略帶有某種奢靡：奶油番茄濃湯、新英格蘭龍蝦、德州肋骨牛肉、四季豆和小圓麵包，最後以法式糕點結束。

　　甘迺迪擔任總統期間，美蘇冷戰仍然持續，而這既是經濟增長也是全球動盪的時代，反而使人們內省反思的精神上揚。他的就職演說「同胞們，不要問國家能為你做些什麼，而要問你可以為國家做些什麼。全世界的公民們，不要問美國會為你做些什麼，應該問我們在一起能為人的自由做些什麼」如今已舉世聞名。雖然在一九六四年慘遭暗殺，總統任期還不到三年，但甘迺迪做為政治家和美國文化偶像遺留的影響力仍在。

左頁與次頁：甘迺迪就職典禮午宴菜單，封面上有與會出席者的簽名，內頁全是白宮供應的餐點

In Honor of

The President of the United States

JOHN FITZGERALD KENNEDY

and

The Vice President of the United States

LYNDON BAINES JOHNSON

Supreme Court Chamber, Capitol Building

Hosts

The Joint Congressional Inaugural Committee

JOHN SPARKMAN, of Alabama, *Chairman*

CARL HAYDEN, of Arizona

STYLES BRIDGES, of New Hampshire

SAM RAYBURN, of Texas

JOHN W. McCORMACK, of Massachusetts

CHARLES A. HALLECK, of Indiana

INAUGURAL LUNCHEON 1961

Cream of Tomato Soup With Crushed Popcorn

Deviled Crabmeat Imperial

*New England Boiled Stuffed Lobster With
Drawn Butter*

Prime Texas Ribs of Beef au jus

String Beans Amandine   *Broiled Tomato*

*Grapefruit and Avocado Sections With
Poppyseed Dressing*

Hot Garlic Bread   *Butterflake Rolls*

Pattiserie Bâteau Blanche

Mints   *Coffee*

就職典禮午宴上，歐巴馬用餐的座位擺置

2009

歐巴馬在白宮的第一餐

海鮮酥皮濃湯

·

鴨肉和雉雞串燒佐什錦蔬菜

·

肉桂蘋果海綿蛋糕

二〇〇九年一月二十日，兩百三十位客人來到白宮參加歐巴馬總統的第一任就職典禮午宴。即將上桌款待他們的餐點靈感來自林肯總統，同時表現了美國歷史即將展開新篇章的樂觀氛圍，還略受美國傳統家庭料理影響。

新總統的談話本身是有史以來最受關注的總統演說之一。受到林肯著名的蓋茲堡演說中「自由的新生」（'A New Birth of Freedom'）一語啟發，美國第四十四任總統談到了希望和國家團結，接著才和客人一同坐下來享用一頓頌揚美國物產的佳餚。

餐點之精美，光從菜餚名稱看不出來。來自維吉尼亞州的外燴公司「美食設計」（Design Cuisine）在宴會前接受《衛報》（The Guardian）採訪時表示，歐巴馬提出的要求是能帶來「『舒適感』，但又不會太精緻、不會太花哨」的料理。這頓飯的第一道菜是林肯最愛的海鮮燉湯，使用了緬因州的龍蝦、扇貝、大蝦和鱈魚，上面蓋著酥皮。接下來是來自加州、聽起來相當傳統的鴨肉和雉雞，搭配加州的蘆筍、胡蘿蔔、球芽甘藍和扁豆，以及黑皮諾葡萄酒，然後是可稱為美國人氣甜點的肉桂蘋果蛋糕。整體菜色既精緻又能滿足大眾口味。

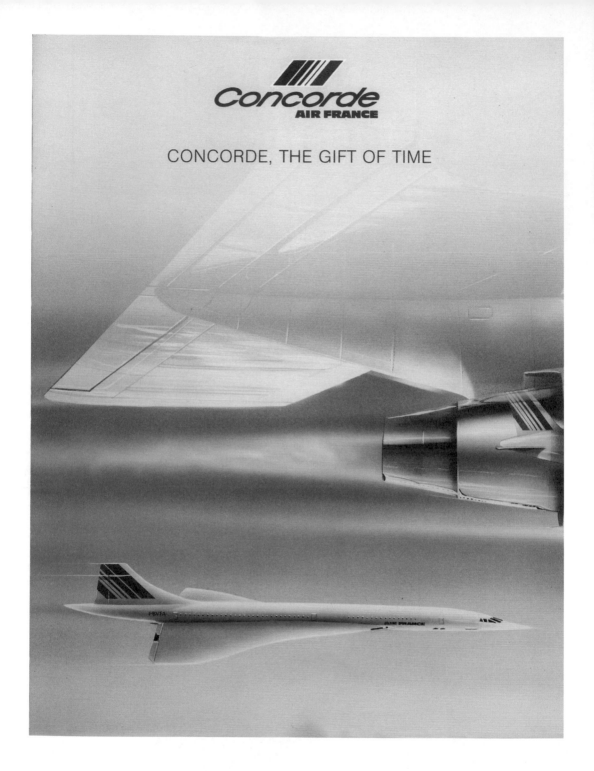

CONCORDE, THE GIFT OF TIME

法國航空協和客機的廣告

催生菜單的社會變化

這一節將提供真正的思維食糧；從菜單本身可以看出文化風氣的轉變、政治決策造成的分歧，以及科技的提升。這些事件彼此雖然千差萬別，但都代表著同一件事——進步——定義這些事件的食物同樣不容小覷。

法國前線的紅十字食堂在列辛頓日（Lexington Day）的晚餐菜色，
這是工作人員為了紀念美國紅十字會會長而準備的

美國紅十字會食堂餐飲

三明治

·

餡餅

·

甜甜圈

　　美國紅十字會最初只在美國境內服務，於重要的交通樞紐或火車站提供免費的餐點和零食給在各州之間移駐的部隊。然而，美國自一九一七年加入第一次世界大戰後，紅十字會的業務很快就擴展到了歐洲，以巴黎為起點開始為美軍服務。

　　紅十字會的規模迅速擴大，以便餵養來自義大利、法國和英國的盟軍。據該組織紀錄，戰爭期間約有五萬五千名女性志工為來自全球近四千萬名士兵服務。為紅十字會工作對這些婦女而言像是某種義不容辭的召喚。沿著前線設置的二十二個食堂所在地全部非常危險，都以廢棄的房舍和棚屋（充其量只要有屋頂就算數）改建而成，婦女們負責烹煮食物，男性志工則負責維護設施。

　　紅十字會食堂除了為經過的饑餓士兵提供三明治、零食、蛋糕、餅乾、甜甜圈和餡餅，幫他們當時少得可憐的口糧加餐，也提供淋浴設施與座位讓他們短暫歇息。這些食堂位於前線、航空營地、醫院，以及部隊持續進出歐洲的駐紮城市。

一九一八年，美國紅十字會食堂的工作人員為駐防法國伊蘇丹（Issoudun）的美國士兵提供咖啡

一九三三年，紐約船長飯店燒烤餐廳（Grill Room）的午餐菜單

1933

禁酒時期的雞尾酒

　　相當諷刺的，「禁酒時期」正是某些流行全球的雞尾酒被發明出來的年代，像是薄荷茱莉普酒、琴費士（gin fizz）、側車（sidecar）和威士忌酸酒（whiskey sour），據說，海鮮類和水果類雞尾酒也是這時創造出來的。

　　從一九二〇年開始一直持續到一九三三年的美國憲法第十八條修正案禁止酒精濃度超過〇‧五％的飲料。關於這項立法所導致的組織犯罪增加已有大量文獻記載且加以美化渲染，但是，那些靠著酒品打出名聲的飯店、酒吧和餐館又受到什麼影響呢？不可能將酒精飲料漲價促使了這些店家從菜單中尋找新的生財之道。

　　將大蝦、龍蝦和螃蟹等甲殼類海產，加上番茄醬、辣椒和（通常會有的）辣根調製而成的辛辣「雞尾酒」醬汁，以及一點點生菜，這源於二十世紀初加州海岸海鮮小吃的組合，就能為正餐之前來一點花俏的變化。

　　既然造型高雅的高腳玻璃杯這段時間似乎無用武之地，水果雞尾酒就成了再次利用它們的完美方式，也讓這種代替開胃酒的產品流行了起來。船長飯店（the Commodore Hotel，現稱君悅酒店〔the Grand Hyatt〕）的菜單提供了螃蟹雞尾酒，紐約的柏克萊酒店（the Berkeley hotel）則派出水果雞尾酒為整頓晚餐打頭陣。

一九四九年十月二十九日，食堂阿姨為學童分送午餐

1944

校園供餐

炸肉片

·

牧羊人派

·

果醬布丁捲

　　英國的全國學校膳食政策（National School Meals Policy）是根據《教育法》（*Education Act*）在一九四四年制定的，意味著有史以來第一次，英國每間學校的孩子都能免費享用午餐和牛奶。此政策於一九四七年全面實施。

　　雖然貧困家庭自一八七九年後就開始獲得糧食供應，不過全國學校膳食政策可是在戰爭陰影下的政治改革時期實行的，為社會大眾邁出正向積極的一步。《多佛快訊》（*Dover Express*）的一篇文章稱這項新做法「受歡迎且有成效」，描述它「每天的菜色都有變化」。事實是，這意味「孩子們能吃到一般家庭配給不到的飯菜，可無限量地自行取用烤牛肉和約克郡布丁，或是水煮羊肉」。

　　在多佛（Dover），年齡較大的孩子輪流負責協助送餐，餐點則在以前的家政中心烹調準備。到了一九五○年代，校園內提供的餐點已經變得有點單調一致，讓午餐主食如炸肉片、牧羊人派、蒸海綿蛋糕淋卡士達醬、果醬布丁捲成為近幾十年來英國飲食文化的象徵。儘管這些餐點可能會勾起某些人的不愉快回憶，近幾年也確實有理由受到監督與檢視，但為了受教權的平等，提供所有人免費餐食仍然是不可或缺的。

The National Health Service

HIS MAJESTY'S STATIONERY OFFICE   6d. NET

一九四七年，國民保健署手冊封面

1948

早期國民保健署的醫院供餐

羊肉派

·

水煮甘藍菜、蕪菁與馬鈴薯

·

焗飯佐梅爾芭蜜桃霜淇淋

　　成立於一九四八年的國民保健署（NHS, National Health Service）是戰後英國史上最重要的社會改革之一。儘管今日醫院供應給形形色色病人的食物豐富多元，國民保健署成立初期由於受到戰後衰疲重振中的經濟和食物配給制影響，能夠提供的餐點相當有限。

　　這種狀況一直持續到一九五四年，此時距離戰爭結束已經很久了。糖、雞蛋、乳酪、肉品和茶葉仍然限額配給，戰爭期間從未定量配給的麵包實際上在一九四六年也被劃入了配給範圍。當時給予病患的餐食只能勉強符合當今營養要求的最低標準，如燉小牛頭、醃魚（kipper）和醫院自家庭園栽種蔬菜等。

　　不像今天由集中的供應商送來，一九四〇年代的醫院供餐是在院內烹調的，飯菜種類多樣，但整體來說反映了當時常見的家庭料理，就是蛋白質和兩種蔬菜。如果有三種，算你走運。

　　儘管約莫七十年過去，飲食潮流早已不同，醫院早餐卻一直沒多大改變，烤麵包和麥片粥從未被踢出菜單，倒是吃牛羊內臟和罐頭魚肉的日子早已遠去了，萬幸。

NASA 太空人使用的餐飲包，其中還有脫水果汁

1969

在太空中用餐

培根塊

·

甜食零嘴

·

咖啡

　　美國的登月之舉也許是二十世紀最具歷史意義的事件之一，太空人阿姆斯壯（Neil Armstrong）和艾德林（Buzz Aldrin）這趟搭乘阿波羅十一號之旅最終達成了史上第一次載人降落，並且想當然地，人類在月球表面的第一頓飯也被他們吃了。

　　然而，這並不是太空中的第一頓晚餐。此榮譽歸於太空人葛倫（John Glenn），他在一九六二年不自覺地成了實驗白老鼠，測試人類是否有可能在零重力下進食。幸運的是，這確實是可能的 —— 葛倫吃下了一管蘋果醬。或許稱不上是美味的一餐，但絕對是一項里程碑。

　　輪到艾德林和阿姆斯壯的時候，事情變得更複雜了些 —— 菜單上有脫水培根塊、桃子、甜食零嘴和葡萄柚鳳梨綜合果汁飲料，再來一杯咖啡完美收尾。太空人在月表的靜海盆地中享用了這頓飯，在月球表面上待了近二十二個小時之後才飛回地球。

　　儘管太空旅行背後的技術或許已不可同日而語，但提供的餐飲並沒有多大改變，菜單上仍可見到培根，令人有些意外。不過，現在的太空人有一百多種菜色可以挑選，有時甚至要提前好幾個月就決定。

催生菜單的社會變化

Aperitifs and Cocktails

Sweet and Dry Vermouth
Campari Soda
Americano . Negroni
Medium Dry Sherry
Dry Martini . Gin . Vodka
Bloody Mary . Old Fashioned . Manhattan
Sours – *Whisky . Gin . Brandy*
Gin Fizz

Highballs – *Whisky . Brandy . Gin . Rum*

Champagne Cocktail

Spirits

Whisky – *Scotch . Bourbon . Rye*
Gin
Vodka

Beers

Ale . Lager

Selection of Soft Drinks

Wines

Champagne
Grand Siècle
or
Heidsieck Dry Monopole 1975

Bordeaux
Château la Dominique 1973
as available

White Burgundy
Chablis 1979

Liqueurs

Remy Martin Napoleon Brandy
Drambuie . Cointreau . Kahlua
Fonseca Bin 27 Port

Jamaica Macanudo cigars

Aperitifs — Champagne

Canapés
Caviar, goose liver pâté and shrimps

Lunch
Déjeuner

Saumon fumé et crabe
*Thin slices of scotch smoked salmon garnished with crab legs
presented with lemon and buttered brown bread*

— * —

Tournedos grillé aux chanterelles
*Prime fillet of beef seared on a hot griddle, served with
sautéed cantharellus mushrooms*

Pâté chaude de gibier
*This English style game pie is prepared from marinated venison,
pheasant, mushrooms and morels baked with a crust of
flaky puff pastry*

Truite Cléopâtre
*A filleted trout, pan fried in butter, garnished with shrimps, capers
and soft roes and finished with nut brown butter*

Légumes
French beans, baby carrots and baked straw potatoes with artichokes

— * —

Salade
*Wafers of avocado pear and apple, flavoured with lemon juice and
fresh mayonnaise*

— * —

Choix de fromage
*A selection of French Camembert, English Stilton and Cheddar
cheese*

— * —

Fraises Romanoff
*Ripe strawberries marinated in orange juice, flavoured with
maraschino and kirsch, mixed with lightly whipped dairy cream*

— * —

Café . Coffee
Served with chocolate mint crisps

一九七八年，從倫敦飛往紐約的協和式客機供餐菜單

1978

協和式客機上吃些什麼

魚子醬

·

英式小羊排

·

草莓奶油薄餅

由於先前提升的創新能力，整個二十世紀無論是空運、海運或鐵道交通，朝奢華風格傾斜已是回不了頭的大勢所趨。儘管首次載客航空旅行一九一四年就已出現，之後的許多年裡，商業飛行仍然頗有上流社會專屬的意味，絕大部分原因當然是價格令人望而生畏，而協和式客機的問世與一九八〇年代的經濟繁榮更讓航空旅行的奢華來到了新境界。

協和式飛機以超音速（準確地說是兩倍音速）飛行。一九七六年至二〇〇三年間，英國航空公司（British Airways）和法國航空（Air France）用協和式飛機載運了超過兩百五十萬名乘客，將倫敦和紐約之間的飛行時間縮短到僅需三個半小時，原本得花上八小時。

協和式客機不僅擁有自己的酒窖，還為乘客提供了包括龍蝦、鵝肝醬和魚子醬，由博古斯（Paul Bocuse）、米歇爾·魯（Michel Roux）和科里根（Richard Corrigan）等大廚設計的標準三道式套餐（前菜、主餐和甜點）。不難想見，協和式客機在倫敦希思洛機場和紐約甘迺迪國際機場之間的首航午餐是多麼高級與奢侈：魚子醬、螃蟹、英式小羊排和草莓奶油薄餅，搭配香檳，接著還有雪茄和干邑白蘭地。

由於機票價格高達八千英鎊，二〇〇〇年代初協和式客機的機票銷量下降，最終在二〇〇三年飛完最後一趟後，結束營運。

英國在二戰時期發起「掘土挖地求勝利」（'Dig for Victory'）運動，
薯仔彼特（Potato Pete）是當時宣傳的熱門角色

料理書的歷史

儘管料理類書籍在當前具有一定的文化地位——有些像是回憶錄、有些如美術畫冊、有些是咖啡桌上擺設用的精美大書——食譜在歷史上的地位卻相當卑微。然而，這些指導手冊反映了種種社會變化，從社會流動、殖民探勘到飲食道德和抽象藝術運動。

MODERN COOKERY,

FOR PRIVATE FAMILIES,

REDUCED TO A SYSTEM OF EASY PRACTICE,

IN A SERIES OF

CAREFULLY TESTED RECEIPTS,

IN WHICH THE PRINCIPLES OF

BARON LIEBIG AND OTHER EMINENT WRITERS

HAVE BEEN AS MUCH AS POSSIBLE APPLIED AND EXPLAINED.

BY ELIZA ACTON.

"It is the want of a scientific basis which has given rise to so many absurd and hurtful methods of preparing food."—DR. GREGORY.

NEWLY REVISED AND MUCH ENLARGED EDITION.
COPIOUSLY ILLUSTRATED.

LONDON:
LONGMANS, GREEN, READER, AND DYER.
1868.

如今已成名著的阿克頓烹飪書籍一八五八年版扉頁

1845

阿克頓的
《私人居家現代烹飪大全》

水煮羊腿佐舌肉片與蕪菁
·
聖誕布丁

伊萊莎·阿克頓（Eliza Acton）被史密斯（Delia Smith）封為「最佳英語食譜作家之一」其實是遭到嚴重的低估，因為無論過去還是現在的美食界，只要提起阿克頓的名字，莫不肅然起敬。她的《私人居家現代烹飪大全》（*Modern Cookery for Private Families*）出版於一八四五年，編著詳盡、介紹全面且非常詳細，是英國烹飪料理書籍的始祖之一。

阿克頓在前言大膽宣告了一句上百位前輩美食作家奉為圭臬的話：「好廚藝才是最經濟省錢的方法。」（Good cookery is the truest economy.）事實上，阿克頓深深感覺新興中產階級有必要享受優質餐飲，因此她說：「正是出身自這些階級的人們勤奮不懈，心智卓越，展現靈動的才華，人類的科學、藝術、文學和整體社會文明才能有所進步，我們都虧欠他們甚多。」

整本書從頭到尾都可感覺阿克頓關注細節的程度幾乎到了有點誇張的地步，甚至連標題旁邊的注釋也是如此。比如水煮羊腿佐舌肉片與蕪菁這道菜，菜名後面的括號內寫「極好的配方」（an excellent receipt）。描述調理手法時也表現出極大的熱情：「將其切出美麗外形，切成保存完好但無損甜美的羊腿。」

這本書也是第一份提到「聖誕」布丁（不同於狄更斯的「李子」布丁）的文獻，並大力擁護英式烹飪──當時人們談起夢幻美食總是不離法國料理。不過，最重要的也許是，阿克頓是向大家倡導飲食應健康營養、美味可口且精心烹製的先驅之一，而且主張無論社會地位或預算多寡都一樣。

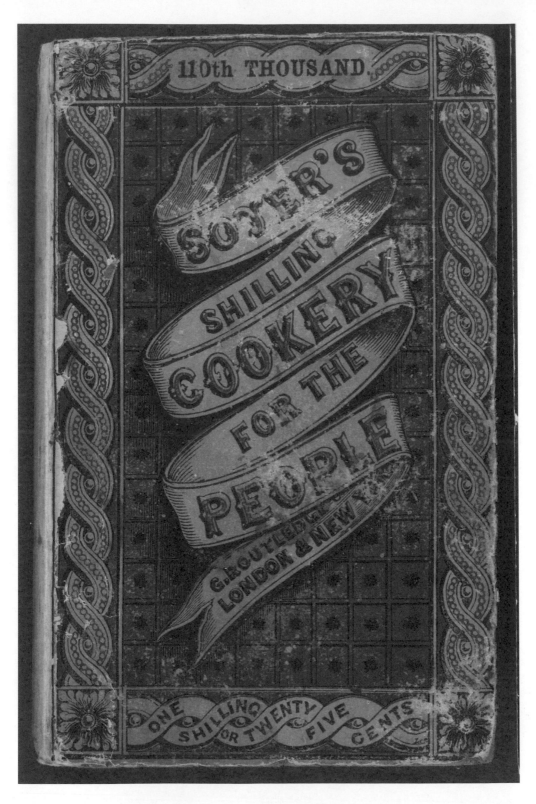

索耶的料理書籍封面相當引人矚目

1854

索耶的庶民料理書

銅板價豌豆湯／簡化版什錦雜燴湯／人人吃得起的李子布丁

　　當烹飪料理寫作的主要目標讀者集中在新興的中產階級，一本能夠滿足他們需求──提供庶民出身者看重的實用知識，兼顧他們在財富、社會地位到手後進而企求的氣質風尚──的食譜，好比索耶（Alexis Soyer）一八五四年撰寫的《人人都能掌握的料理：樸實烹飪和家計經濟新主張》（*Shilling Cookery for the People: An Entirely New System of Plain Cookery and Domestic Economy*）就來得正是時候，大受好評。

　　來自法國的索耶在法國上流社會的廚房待過一段時間，後來才到英國為王公貴族掌廚，以他的創新之舉博得名聲與美譽。索耶以其廚房設計而聞名，將瓦斯燃料、可調節爐具和效能更高的冷藏系統引入許多家庭，但他對社會公義同樣滿懷熱忱，從這層意義上來說，他真正稱得上是一位革新主義者。據說索耶提出了「慈善廚房」（soup kitchen）的概念，並向大英政府提議以這種方式來幫助愛爾蘭大饑荒的災民。這項計畫後來於一八四七年開始在都柏林推行。

　　索耶先前寫過《索耶愛心烹飪》（*Soyer's Charitable Cookery*）和《現代主婦》（*The Modern Homewife*）等書，《人人都能掌握的料理》則專為買不起廚房設備或昂貴食材的人而寫。這本書內容豐富詳盡，除了大讚牛尾的營養成分高，價格不貴又能連用好多餐，也哀嘆香料和菜葉未被充分使用而導致食物浪費，還介紹了他那道真材實料、「不為百萬富翁，而是為百萬民眾調整過」的李子布丁配方。儘管收錄了像是銅板價豌豆湯（Cheap Pea Soup）和簡化版什錦雜燴湯（Hodge-Podge）──用羊肉碎渣製成的燉菜──這種相當傳統的英國菜，但索耶也確實添加了些許法式風情，書中不但有醬汁和簡易沙拉的專屬章節，還鼓勵多多使用「幾品脫奶油」。

　　從廚房設備的插圖到方便迅速的聖誕節菜單，甚至是他為參與克里米亞戰爭的英軍所開發的菜色，在索耶卷帙浩繁的食譜書寫中，到處都看得到他對飲食和「民眾」的熱愛。正如他自己說的，「吃飯不喝酒，或者光喝酒不吃飯，都會讓人早早上西天」。

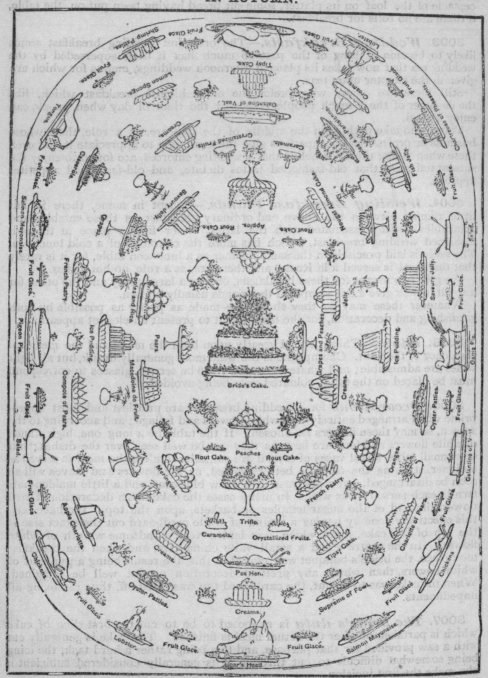

3008.—WEDDING BREAKFAST FOR LARGE PARTY IN AUTUMN.

Note.—This breakfast is suitable for a very large party. The list of dishes, which can easily be reduced, will be found on page 1321.

上圖：《比頓夫人的家務寶典》書中，擺置完善的餐桌插圖

次頁：十六人座的餐桌擺置

1861

《比頓夫人的家務寶典》

龍蝦沙拉

·

小麵餅佐牛羊內臟

·

波爾多烤乳鴿

·

小火腿舒芙蕾

·

炸馬鈴薯球

·

醋栗奶油布丁

　　《比頓夫人的家務寶典》的內容反映了過去一百七十五年來的社會史，可說是最重要的出版品之一。儘管作者早在一八六五年便離世，這部頁數破千的厚書銷量卻超過了兩百萬冊，今日仍舊印行發售。這本書源自連載了二十四期的雜誌專欄，作者伊莎貝拉·比頓（Isabella Beeton）從二十一歲起就在丈夫的雜誌上撰寫專欄。她在序言中談到自己的創作動機：「我一直認為，造成家庭紛爭的原因，莫過於主婦燒飯不好吃、打掃不整潔。」從如何面試負責各種家務的合適僕人、是否帶著狗出門參加社交活動，到烤出完美香草海綿蛋糕的方法、肉片該怎麼切最適合煮湯等，你能想到的任何家務，書中都指示了正確做法。菜單規劃亦然。書中建議的「美味正式午宴」菜色，照今天的標準看來非常重口味，包括了羊雜碎、烤野味和可愛迷人的「炸馬鈴薯球」。

　　後來人們發現，大部分食譜都是比頓夫人從其他烹飪書籍抄來的。沒錯，相當具有道德爭議。然而維多利亞時代的社會流動性之高，過往難以想像，此時新興的中產階級婦女尚在摸索適應，比頓夫人的書確實為她們提供了簡易安全的指南。

《英格蘭與澳大利亞烹飪書》扉頁

1864

澳洲第一本烹飪書

烤袋熊

·

口腔漱福

·

滑溜鮑勃

一八六〇年代，正當英國家家戶戶開始依循《比頓夫人的家務寶典》一板一眼的指示，同屬大英國協的澳洲同胞即將和自己國家的食譜巨著打照面了——由塔斯馬尼亞農民阿伯特（Edward Abbott）撰寫、書名頗吸引人的《英格蘭與澳大利亞烹飪書：不分貴賤的全民食譜》（*The English and Australian Cookery Book: Cookery for the Many, as Well as the Upper Ten Thousand*）。

位於南半球的澳大利亞典型料理風格就是混融，阿伯特的食譜可謂最早的範例，他採用歐洲料理烹煮、醃漬和蒸餾的原理，應用在澳洲本地動物和食材上。得到的結果？烤袋熊、糖蜜醃製的豬油和一種用白蘭地、水和糖混合調製成的「口腔漱福」（shuvin-the-mouth），以及其他一千道菜餚。

出生於雪梨的阿伯特致力於與人（即使是最貧窮卑微者）分享想法，樂此不疲之餘，還希望以最好的方式記錄家鄉當地食材，書中甚至有一章專門談剩菜剩飯，希望減少食物浪費，並大談如何料理袋鼠每個身體部位——包括尾巴。

這本書最初由倫敦的出版商發行，二〇一四年正值此書出版一百五十周年時又再刷印行。書中食譜毫無意外地引來大量關注，特別是「滑溜鮑勃」（slippery bob）這道菜，就是用鴯鶓油脂烹煮的袋鼠腦。

一九三二年，《未來派食譜》封面

1932

未來主義烹飪

立體派蔬菜拼盤
·
不死鱒魚
·
月光之約

　　二十世紀初的未來主義運動是由飽受爭議的藝術家馬里內蒂（Filippo Tommaso Marinetti）發起的，排斥歷史和傳統，崇尚未來，欲探索未知事物和快速進展的科技。但這和食物有關嗎？

　　一九三〇年，馬里內蒂與未來派畫家菲莉莎（Fillìa）一同擬定《未來主義烹飪宣言》（*Manifesto of Futurist Cooking*），隨後在一九三二年出版了《未來派食譜》（*The Futurist Cookbook*）。後者其實是一本規則設定集，鼓勵人們拒絕已經嘗試和檢驗過的食物調理方式，轉而選擇從食材到外觀都能挑戰且激發想像力的菜餚。

　　要滿足未來主義宣言的宗旨得做到十一項關鍵要求，其中包括：用餐時有香氛和音樂相伴，且每道菜搭配的都不一樣；放棄刀叉；利用科技簡化備餐步驟等，最後同時最受爭議的則是從飲食中排除義大利麵。另外，馬里內蒂也建議禁止在餐桌上聊政治，這或許是書中較為明智的建議之一。

　　菜單包括了立體派風格的配菜，例如將蔬菜切成比一立方公分還小的蔬菜丁；魚類料理如「不死鱒魚」（Immortal Trout）是一尾塞滿堅果的魚，裹在小牛肝中後再油炸，有刺激味蕾的意味；最後是聽起來很美味的甜點「月光之約」（Dates in Moonlight），其實是義大利瑞可塔軟酪（ricotta）佐棗子果泥，冰鎮保存直到上餐前才解凍。

史上第一場未來主義餐宴的照片

一九五四年，《好管家菜色全書》（*Good Housekeeping Book of Menus*）的秋季料理

1936

《好管家》

鮭魚、義大利麵與番茄燉鍋／奶油玉米

·

加熱菜捲／鳳梨與紅蘋果沙拉

·

各式乳酪與脆餅／茶

　　《好管家》（*Good Housekeeping*）是美國麻薩諸塞州發行的雜誌，這份兩星期出刊一次的讀物剛開始並不起眼，卻在過去一百三十四年間成長為全球事業體。這本雜誌的定位是協助女性做家事的指南，內容括及烹飪、流行時尚、商品貨物，當然還有家務，並在短短幾年內擁有超過三十萬名讀者。

　　一九○○年代初期，電力的出現意味著家庭生活已經發生轉變，新的電器產品、生活更輕鬆、工作更迅速。為了回應此趨勢，《好管家》建立了現今簡稱為 GHI 的「好管家評測室」（Good Housekeeping Institute），一間針對電器進行測試、為讀者提供評比意見的實驗室。

　　《好管家》的內容始終是社會變遷的指標，從一九一四年速食餐飲的危險性到爭取更多聯邦政府預算投入母嬰照護的宣傳運動，雜誌都曾談到，飲食編輯馬許（Dorothy Marsh）寫的〈給忙碌職業婦女們的快速晚餐料理建議〉（'Dinners without Delay for Busy and Business Housekeepers'）則回應了愈來愈多女性外出工作的情況。馬許這份既經濟又實用的菜單早早預告了一場排除速食快餐、免下車餐廳和微波加熱餐這類一九五○年代美國飲食代名詞的社會變化。在這篇一九三六年的文章中，馬許分享的主要祕訣包括：將即食調理包與用手邊食材即興烹煮的菜餚結合在一起；每星期開始前就規劃好一周菜單；馬鈴薯和蔬菜都多煮一些，準備兩頓飯食用的量；將食物直接放在用餐盤子上，免得還要多洗那些上菜用的鍋盤──全都言之有理。

PARTY MENUS

DINNER PARTY 1
Consommé Julienne
Roast Pheasant
Bread Sauce   Fried Crumbs
Game Chips
Green Salad with Tangerines
Peach Liqueur Flan

DINNER PARTY 2
Oxtail Soup
Fried Scallops
Grilled Beefsteak
Hot Potato Salad
Sauté of Peas
Strawberry Mousse
Sponge Fingers
Cheese Meringues

DINNER PARTY 3
Glazed Paupiettes of Sole
Roast Duck
Green Peas   Roast Potatoes
Apple Sauce   Orange Salad
Chocolate Refrigerator Cake
Angels on Horseback

CHRISTMAS DINNER 1
Artichoke Soup
Roast Turkey
Sausages   Bread Sauce
Brussels Sprouts
Christmas Pudding
Brandy Butter
Mince Pies

CHRISTMAS DINNER 2
Cream of Chestnut Soup
Turkey Soufflé Pie
Mushroom Fritters
Potato Croquettes
Flaming Peaches
Lemon Meringue Pie

NEW YEAR BUFFET
Ragoût of Goose with Chestnuts
Prawn Patties
Chicken and Tongue in Aspic
Asparagus Rolls
Nut and Cherry Trifle
Fruit Salad and Peach Ice Cream
Pineapple Sponge
Individual Trifles
Apricots in Liqueur
Petits Fours

DINNER PARTY 4
Marrow Cream Soup
Chicken and Ham Vol-au-Vent
Asparagus à la Crème
Lyonnaise Potatoes
Orange Soufflé
Bananas au Rhum
Sardine Strips

DINNER PARTY 5
French Tomato Soup
Salmon Trout Mayonnaise
Roast Parsley Potatoes
Summer Salad   Beetroot Salad
Cherry Flan   Baked Alaska

[121]

晚宴菜單與圖片，出自一九五四年《好管家菜色全書》

英國糧食部的宣傳廣告「吃得聰明好作戰」（'Wise Eating in Wartime'）

1940

戰爭時期的菜色

培根肉片鍋

·

高麗菜絲

·

餃子淋糖漿

德國在大西洋海戰採取的策略——攻擊運往英國的進口貨物船隻——使得英國糧食部於一九三九年針對某些食物實施全國定量配給制度，這套制度對某些食材持續列管了十五年。本地種植的蔬菜和麵包不受限制，但肉類和乳製品（如培根、其他紅肉和奶油）則受到嚴格管制，糖也是。

到了一九四二年，乳酪、雞蛋、茶葉、咖啡、餅乾和水果罐頭仍名列管制清單，政府也發布了一系列傳單來幫助百姓腦筋急轉彎，利用有限的供應物資發揮創意，好比：用馬鈴薯和蔬菜撐出菜餚豐盛場面，將過期麵包用在甜品和鹹味菜餚以避免浪費，用果醬和轉化糖漿（golden syrup）*代替糖等。

一餐飯的組成內容因此大幅轉變，影響持續至今。舉例來說，僅用少量油脂加上增添甜味的轉化糖漿所製成的餃子餐，在接下來幾十年成了學校餐點的固定菜色。數百份傳單裡寫的都是糧食部編寫的食譜，對英國的烹飪方式產生的影響至今未退。

以下兩頁是倫敦市中心法式小酒館「梅李小館」（Maison Prunier）的菜單，清楚標示了哪些餐點是限量配給的（每人只能點一份），哪些未受配給限制（可以盡情享用）。他們還提供「空襲時分午餐」（Air Raid Lunch）和「燈火管制叫車服務」（black-out taxi service），幫助顧客在倫敦大轟炸時期通過黑暗的街道安全返家。

＊將甘蔗或甜菜汁精製成糖的過程中，或者在用酸處理糖溶液時的產物。用於各種烘焙食品和甜點，外觀與蜂蜜相似。

MENU

NO COVER CHARGED
(AUCUN PLAT N'EST SERVI POUR DEUX)

HORS d'OEUVRE

A LONDRES
MAISON PRUNIER
St. James's Restaurant Ltd
72 St. James's Street
Telephone Regent 1373-1374

TASTE OUR WINES
by glass
Anjou, Graves, Maconnais 1/9
Bordeaux Rouge 1/9
Champagne St. James 3/-

COQUILLAGES ET HUITRES

NOS SPECIALITES

Huitres Frites........ les 3 2/9
    ,, au Gratin........ ,, 2/9
    ,, sur croûton.... ,, 2/9
    ,, à l'Américaine ,, 2/9
    ,, en Brochette.. ,, 2/9
Potage aux Huitres........ 6/-
Variété Prunier (6 oysters) 5/6
Potage de Fruits de Mer 4/6

Bigorneaux ....la portion 1/-
Moules Parquées........ la douz. 1/6
Portugaises .... la douz. 5/6
L'Assiette Saintongeaise 3/6
L'Assiette Blackout or Air Raid 3/6

Brittany petites.............la douz. 7/-
Brittany supérieures.... ,, 9/6
Natives petites............... ,, 8/-
Natives supérieures........ ,, 10/-
Natives extra................ ,, 12/-
(See full explanations on other page.)

PRUNIER SPECIAL GREEN OYSTERS
Petites......................... 8/-
Supérieures................. 10/-
Extra.......................... 11/-

FUMAISONS, COCKTAILS

Saumon fumé.........................3/-
Crevette Cocktail......................3/-
Crabe Cocktail.........................3/-
Oyster Cocktail........................3/6

LE PLATEAU PRUNIER

Petit Sandwich Beurre d'Anchois
Petite Coquille salade de Crabe ....
Petite Coquille Crevettes Paprika
Petite coquille, sauce verte...
Fine Bouche de Saumon Fumé
} 3/-

CAVIAR

Caviar de Saumon.... la cuiller.... 3/6
Caviar Pressé....................... 4/6
Caviar Frais Russe Sevruga........ 7/-
Caviar Frais Russe Oscietre........ 9/-
Sandwich de Caviar Frais......... 1/3

DIVERS

Terrine de Lièvre.....................3/6

Foie Gras à la Gelée de Porto 5/-

FROIDS
Potted Shrimps...........la portion 2/6
Bouquet.................... ,, ,, 3/-
CHAUDS
St. Jacques Prunier................ 3/6
St. Jacques Marinière.............. 4/-
St. Jacques Rochelaise............ 4/6

COQUILLAGES AND CRUSTACES
Crabe Mexicaine..................... 3/-
Crabe Dressé Mayonnaise ... 4/-
MOULES MARINIERE 3/-
Pilaff de Moules au Curry... 3/6
Pilaff de Crabe Américaine... 4/6
Pilaff de Crevettes Valencienne.. 4/6

Petit Homard Rémoulade........ 4/6
¡ Langouste Mayonnaise........ 5/6

Homard Thermidor... (1 per.) 5/-
Homard Grillé......................5/6
Homard Américaine.......... 5/6
Homard Newburg................ 6/-

OEUFS

Œuf en Gelée...............................1/9

Omelette au Caviar............... 3/9

POTAGES

Consommé Celestine................1/9

Bisque de Homard................... 2/6
Soupe aux Moules................... 2/6

Potage Parisienne..................... 2/6

BY AGREEMENT WITH THE MINISTRY OF FOOD, ONLY ONE DISH OF MEAT OR POULTRY, OR GAME OR FISH MAY BE SERVED AT A MEAL (MEAT INCLUDING OFFALS) AND BE SELECTED FROM THE FOLLOWING ITEMS:

POISSON
Le Poisson du Chef ....See "TODAY"
STEAK DE TURBOT PARISIENNE 4/-

Hareng Grillé Sce. Moutarde .. 2/6

Whitebaits Diables................. 3/-
Merlan Crawford.................... 3/-

Grillade au Fenouil................. 4/-
BOUILLABAISSE 4/6
Raie au Beurre Noir................3/6
Truite Meunière.....................4/-

Barbue au Four 4/-

Sole Grillée......................... 5/9
Filets de Sole Prunier.............. 5/9

ENTREES, GRILLADE ET ROTS
Le Plat du Gourmet........ "See TODAY"

2 Côtes d'Agneau.................. 3/6
Côte de Mouton ou Veau........... 4/-
Rognons Grillés Vert - Pré .. 3/6
(Toutes les Grillades sont garnies Pommes Bataille)

Pilaff de Volaille au Curry.... 3/6
¡ Poularde au Riz Suprême (2 pers) 12/-

Entrecôte Minute 4/-
Tournedos Beurre d'Anchois.... 4/6
Filet Boston (6 Huîtres)........... 7/-

GIBIER
Perdreau Rôti....................... 10/6
Bécasse Flambée.................... 12/6
Faisan Rôti........................ 15/-

¡ Perdreau aux Choux..............5/6
Canard Sauvage au Porto........ 12/-
,, ,, à la Presse... 15/-

Civet de Lièvre..................... 4/6
Rable de Lièvre Sce. Poivrade 10/-

FROIDS
Langue............................... 2/6
Jambon Froid....................... 2/6

Mayonnaise de Volaille St.James 5/6

Poulet, la cuisse................... 5/6
Poulet, l'Aile...................... 6/6

LEGUMES
Haricots Verts au Beurre 2/-
Purée d'Epinards.................. 2/-

Salade de Saison: 1/3

Choux Fleurs Sautés............... 2/-

Salade Panachée, Salade M-C-B 1/6

Petits Pois Etouffés Française.. 1/-
Champignons Grillés Sur Toast 2/6

Salade de Légumes 2/-

FROMAGES
Cheddar, — Cheshire 1/3

Stilton 1/6

A SPECIALITY; Cœur Mousseline 1/6

ENTREMETS ET DESSERTS
Pôt de Crème; Chocolat, Vanille 1/6
Fruits Rafraîchis au Marasquin 2/6
Tarte aux Fruits................... 2/6

Glace Vanille ou Fraise 2/-
Mousse Glacée Chocolat 2/3
Mousse Glacée au Rhum 2/6

Coupe Jack 2/6
Crêpes à l'Orange 3/6
Poire Nelusko 3/6

FRUITS DE SAISON
GRAPE FRUIT 1/6
POIRE 2/-

CAFE FILTRE 1/-
   *
CAFE DECAFEINE 1/3

Open the Whole Year round — on **Sundays** for **Lunch** a 12-30, **Dinner** at 7

"TOUT CE QUI VIENT DE LA MER — EVERYTHING COMING FROM THE SEA"

(margin left: Not Rationed — Only one dish can be selected from these items. — Not Rationed)

梅李小館的戰時菜單

A few explanations about some French names on the Menu

OYSTERS
Brittany Petites and Supérieures: French Oysters re-laid in English Waters   **Natives:** English bred Oysters
Prunier Green Special: Oysters bred in England but very similar to French Green Marennes
Assiette Saintongeaise: 6 small Brittany served with a hot sausage   **Portugaises:** Portuguese oysters re-laid in England
Assiette Black-out or Air Raid: 3 Portuguese - 3 small Brittany

COCKTAILS   SHELLFISH   SMOKED FISH
Crevettes Cocktail: Shrimp Cocktail   **Bigorneaux:** Winkles   **Saumon Fumé:** Smoked Salmon
Crabe Cocktail: Crab Cocktail   **Moules Parquées:** Raw Mussels

CAVIAR
Caviar de Saumon: Made with Salmon Roes   **Caviar Russe Sevruga:** Fresh Caviar but with smaller eggs than Oscietre
Caviar Pressé: Pressed Caviar   **Caviar Russe Oscietre:** Bigger egg caviar

DIVERS
Terrine de Lièvre: Hare Pâte
Foie Gras à la Gelée de Porto: Goose Liver served with Jelly made with Port and Truffles

Not
Rat-
CRUSTACES
Crabe Mexicaine: Crab meat, lettuce served in crab shell
ioned   **Crabe Dressé Mayonnaise:** Dressed Crab   **Langouste:** Crawfish   **Bouquet:** Prawns
Pilaff: Rice cake stuffed with Crab, or Shrimps or Mussels and served with American, Newburg, Valencienne or Curry Sauce.
Homard Thermidor: Lobster Meat, Truffles, Mushroom Sauce on half Lobster shell.
Homard Newburg: Lobster with Cream Sauce Sherry, Truffles   **Homard grillé:** Broiled Lobster.
St. Jacques Prunier: Scollops served in a shell with cream sauce   **Mariniere:** Scollops with white wine sauce, Shallot and Parsley
Rochelaise: Served in a shell with the same butter as for Snail
Moules Marinière: Mussels cooked with white wine, chopped onions and Parsley

EGGS
Oeuf en gelée: Egg enrobed in Jelly.
Omelette Caviar: Omelette with caviar.

SOUPS
Consommé Celestine: Consommé relieved with chopped pancakes   **Bisque de Homard:** Lobster Soup hot or cold
Soup aux Moules: Mussel soup   **Potage de Fruits de Mer:** Cream soup with cooked Oysters, Mussels
Potage Parisienne: Leaks and Potatoe Soup

FISH Cold Dishes
Steak de Turbot Parisienne: Cold Turbot in Jelly served with Tomatoes, Vegetable Salad

FISH Hot Dishes
Hareng Grillé Sauce Moutarde: Grilled Herring served with Hollandaise sauce, with slight a mixture of mustard
Grillade au Fenouil: Common fish grilled with fennel in front of client, as prepared in the South of France.
Raie au Beurre Noir: Skate cooked in burnt butter
Bouillabaisse: A variety of Fish with Tomatoes and Saffron Sauce.
Barbue au Four: Brill with White Wine and Cream Sauce
Sole Grillée: Grilled Sole served with melted butter
Filets de Sole Prunier: Sole, Poached Oysters, Truffles, Sauce with White Wine and Cream
Rat-   **Varieté Prunier:** A selection of Oysters cooked in 6 different ways served in shells

MEAT AND POULTRY
ioned   **Poularde au Riz Suprême:** Boiled Chicken, its stock thickened with Cream, served with rice.
Tournedos au Beurre d'Anchois: Tournedos served with butter mixed with Anchovy Sauce.
Filet Boston: Tournedos with Oysters and Hollandaise Sauce   **Pilaff de Volaille au Curry:** Rice Cake stuffed with Chicken Curry Sauce
Mayonnaise de Volaille St. James's: Sliced Chicken with Mayonnaise, Lettuce Salad, Tomatoes, Eggs and Olives

GAME
Perdreau Rôti: Roast Partridge
Demi Perdreau aux Choux: ½ Partridge served with cabbage, sausage and bacon
Civet de Lièvre: Jugged Hare   **Râble de Lièvre:** Roast Saddle of Hare served with mashed chestnuts and Marinade Sauce
Canard Sauvage au Porto: Wild duck served with a port sauce
   „   „   **à la Presse:** to replace the French Rouennais à la Presse served with cooked apples and chipped potatoes
Bécasse Woodcock singed with Brandy

Not
VEGETABLES
Purée d'Epinards: Mashed Spinach   **Choux Fleurs:** Cauliflowers
Haricots Verts: French Beans.   **Laitue:** Lettuce   **Petits Pois:** Peas
Salade Panachée: a variety of salad or Lettuce with Eggs and Tomatoes   **Champignons:** Mushrooms
Rat-   **Salade M-C-B:** Mixture of corn salad, beetroot and Celery

SWEETS
ioned   **Crêpes a l'Orange:** Pancakes similar to Crêpe Suzette cooked with butter and orange, a drop of Triple Sec Liqueur.
Poire Nelusko: A pear served on a lid of vanilla ice dressed with hot chocolat sauce

When at Prunier ask for particulars of:-

Treasure Trove in Tins – Prunier's Specialities in tins for Home and Abroad — see leaflet

On Prendra ("One Will Take") Service   see tariff – REGent 2615.

Air Raid Lunch 8/6   -   -   4 COURSES INCLUDING
Black-Out Dinner (from 6 p.m.)   **10/6** {   Oysters

BLACK-OUT TAXI SERVICE AVAIVABLE TO AND FROM PRUNIER'S

Open on Sundays for Lunch at 12-30 and Dinner – 7 p.m.

一九六〇年，帕頓的《彩頁食譜》封面

1960

帕頓的《彩頁食譜》

騎馬的惡魔
·
騎馬的天使
·
切達起司條
·
帽子別針

　　今日的烹飪書籍充斥著精緻又生動活潑的佳餚美照，對自家燒飯的人宛如可望不可及的夢想指南，但從前這類書籍都是純文字輔以怪異的黑白插圖，直到一九六〇年英國美食作家帕頓（Marguerite Patten）的開創性著作《彩頁食譜》（*Cookery in Colour*）出版，料理書籍的呈現才完全改觀。

　　就這個意義而言，《彩頁食譜》是一本改變一切的書，到了一九六九年，它的銷量已超過一百萬冊，但這不是帕頓初試啼聲並獲得回響的作品。帕頓在第二次世界大戰期間就為英國糧食部擬定食譜，教民眾如何將少得可憐的食物限量配額做最充分的利用，比如蔬菜炒蛋、鹽漬牛肉炸麵糰（corned-beef fritter）和素麵鴨（mock duck）。

　　由哈姆林出版社（Hamlyn）推出的《彩頁食譜》匯集了一千則食譜和烹飪訣竅，自稱是「能應付任何情境的百科全書」。帕頓在引言中巧妙點出：「一餐飯成不成功，重點在於對眼球的吸引力。食物應該既美味又好看。」在娛樂性這章中有一道菜成功說明了這點，就是名字相當奇特、內含切達起司條和香腸捲的「帽子別針」（hat pins）*。

---

*混和香腸絞肉、燕麥、雞蛋與牛奶製成的小肉球，裹上醬汁後插在取食用的小籤上。

1054 SANDWICHES WITH A DIFFERENCE

Never say sandwiches are dull. This picture shows a variety of sandwiches which are suitable even for the most special occasion.

Try: *Sandwich cones* Fresh bread moulded round cream horn cases. Fill with soft cheese, decorated with nuts and sliced olives, and garnish with salami slices

Card Sandwiches Bread cut into fancy shapes with a pastry cutter

Sandwich Gateau etc. See Recipe No.

Make sure your bread is fresh, and the filling moist. Press top and bottom layer of bread firmly together so that the sandwich does not come apart.

By itself, a plate of sandwiches does not look very exciting. But garnishes can make all the difference. Instead of the conventional parsley try halved tomatoes, mandarin oranges, watercress, prawns, cocktail onions, radish flowers — with suitable sandwiches all these garnishes look attractive and can be eaten too.

Serve a light white wine or fruit cup with a sandwich

《彩色烹飪》裡的派對菜單

1055 HAT PINS

8 oz. sausage meat	3 tablespoons
1 beaten egg	quick cooking
1¼ tablespoons milk	rolled oats

For glazing:

¼ tablespoon brown sugar	2 tablespoons fruit juice
3 teaspoons flour	(canned)
¼ teaspoon mustard	¼ tablespoon vinegar
powder	1¼ tablespoons lemon or
3 cloves	orange juice

Mix sausage meat, rolled oats, egg and milk. Chill. Make approximately 32 balls and bake in a shallow dish (325—350°F. — Gas Mark 3) for 30 minutes. Drain off fat. Combine ingredients for glazing. Cook for a few minutes or until slightly thickened. Dip the balls in the glazing. Fix on to cocktail sticks and allow to drain.

1056 MINIATURE PANCAKES

Fill tiny pancakes with creamed chicken or fish. Keep hot until ready to serve. Garnish with peeled shrimps.

1057 SAUSAGE ROLLS

6 oz. flaky pastry	8 oz. sausage meat
	egg yolk or milk to glaze

Roll pastry into a long strip. Form the meat into a long roll and place down one side of the pastry. Fold over and seal edges. Make slits across the top and cut into tiny rolls. Brush with milk or egg yolk and bake in a very hot oven (475°F. — Gas Mark 8) for 15—20 minutes.

1058 HOT BACON COCKTAIL SNACKS

Prepare these earlier in the day — pop into the oven as your guests arrive if you have no means of keeping them hot. Cook for 15 minutes in moderately hot oven, or 25 minutes if covered by foil. If you have a hotplate then just transfer them, when cooked, to a serving dish with absorbent kitchen paper underneath so you can prevent their being greasy, and keep on the hotplate so that guests can help themselves. Put firm cocktail sticks through centre of each roll. These snacks can be grilled or fried instead of being cooked in the oven.

1059 Bacon Frankfurters

Wrap small pieces of streaky bacon round cocktail Frankfurter sausages or portions of large sausages. For variety insert fingers of cheese or a small piece of crisp celery in the Frankfurter sausages.

1060 Cheddar Fingers

Wrap small pieces of bacon round fingers of Cheddar cheese, making certain the cheese is completely covered so that it is easy to eat.

1061 DEVILS ON HORSEBACK

Wrap small pieces of bacon round cooked prunes. If wished put a small piece of liver pâté in the centre of each prune.

1062 ANGELS ON HORSEBACK

Wrap small pieces of bacon round well seasoned oysters.

1063 JAFFA ROLLS

Wrap small pieces of bacon round segments of Jaffa oranges. Brush with little butter before cooking.

The George Bernard Shaw Vegetarian Cook Book

Pan

Illustrated

Mrs Alice Laden
Edited by R. J. Minney

蕭伯納的管家寫的彩色封面食譜

1974

蕭伯納的素食料理書

乳酪芹菜派

·

酪梨柳橙沙拉

·

女王布丁

　　廣受讚譽的劇作家蕭伯納（Bernard Shaw）從二十五歲開始直到九十四歲去世，都堅定地奉行素食主義。他為自己選擇的飲食方式提供了詩意的解釋，說雪萊（Percy Shelley）的詩作〈伊斯蘭的反抗〉（'The Revolt of Islam'）「使我察覺自己的飲食方式多麼殘忍」，詩中有言：「再也不讓鳥獸的鮮血汨汨，如毒汁湧流，沾染人類的筵席。」

　　然而，蕭伯納的女管家拉登（Alice Laden）過世後才出版的食譜中，對此似乎另有解釋，表示他吃素也許是不得不然。原來蕭伯納還是年輕作家時幾乎一文不名，與母親同住，每天步行到大英博物館寫作，在小巷旁的素食小餐館吃飯飽腹比較划算。無論真正的原因是什麼，滴酒不沾的蕭伯納唯一的「罪惡飲食」似乎是糖。拉登說，他經常將糖「一勺一勺塞進嘴裡」。

　　拉登的亡夫生前是位嚴格的素食主義者，因此她對無肉料理下過多年苦功，後來偶然來到蕭伯納家，在其妻生命最後幾個月擔任看護。蕭伯納很喜歡拉登燒的菜，便說服她留下來當廚子，直到蕭伯納於八年後去世。拉登禁止蕭伯納干涉廚房事務和菜單規劃，每天菜色都玩出新花樣。

　　即使是限量配給那幾年，蕭伯納也從不吝於購買進口蔬果，因此能在三道式午餐和兩道式晚餐大啖美食，像是法式焗烤和烘焙糕點，還有咖哩和燉菜。其中值得注意的佳餚如乳酪芹菜派、番茄扇貝、米飯和扁豆炸酥餅、酪梨柳橙沙拉、女王布丁與檸檬冰沙，兩頓飯之間還有蜂蜜甜味蛋糕。

DESSERTS
甜點

甜點就是歌頌浮誇、歌頌創意、歌頌狂歡。本章的菜單恰好反映了這一點，充滿了令人瞠目結舌的著名盛宴、帶著頹廢氣息的最後一餐以及過去兩百年內為知名藝術家、作家和音樂家帶來靈感的餐點。我們在前面兩章已經看到食物如何展現其開拓性並形成社會變革的指標，這一章裡，從一八三七年白宮舉行的起司慶典、王爾德和柯南‧道爾在朗廷酒店享用的罪惡美食晚餐，到貓王夫妻的早餐婚宴，以及法國總統密特朗針對最後一餐提出的古怪要求，食物展現了其娛樂、榮耀或誘惑的功能。

最後一任俄羅斯沙皇加冕典禮的菜單

著名的盛宴

狂歡和盛宴是天生一對，如果想表現行為放縱、奢華享樂，佳餚美饌經常是最強的形象展示。從達爾文在牛津的豪華餐宴到貓王的美國南方風格早餐婚宴，都收錄在以下談論的菜單中——若論鋪張揮霍，個個不遑多讓。

Bill of Fare for

His Majesty's Dinner on Christmas Day 1755.

First Course.

Top Dish.

The House of a Bird with the Life and Death of a Calf, season'd with Lord Mayor's pride and Welchman's Delight, and garnish'd with an Old Woman of ninety odd. This was a Soup.

The Remove.

The Fleetest Conveyance.

Stars broil'd with Lawyers fees for Sauce; garnish'd with Horses.

Bottom Dishes.

Fragments of the preserve of Rome in a pye.

The Sign of the going out of March divided with the Debtors Security, Smart Wine, and the produce of a Walking Stick.

Side Dishes.

Eternal Spikes broil'd.

The Impostors Easing ragou'd.

Second Course.

Furrows roasted.

An unruly Member chopt small & mixd with reason, and confin'd in a Courtiers promise.

The Top of Corn roasted.

These were the Top, bottom, & middle Dishes.

Side Dishes.

Colour'd Boards fricaseed with Stationer's Ware.

The best of a Fish burnt

A Ragou of Shops, with the Original of Eternal spikes and the sweet Support of Life cut small.

一七五五年，喬治二世的聖誕節餐宴菜單，大英圖書館存檔副本

1755

喬治二世的聖誕節餐宴菜單

鬱卒湯

·

水煮人肉的高級部位

·

一陣輕風的初次

　　許多人相信聖誕節傳統始於狄更斯。沒錯，《小氣財神》（*A Christmas Carol*）裡確實找得到許多關於聖誕節習俗起源的解答，狄更斯和他同時代的維多利亞人的確最早實行那些如今充滿象徵意義的聖誕節習俗，比如以樹木裝飾客廳、在餐桌旁玩拉炮等，不過聖誕節吃大餐的傳統比這些更久遠。事實上，不只食物，到處可見的節日笑話和謎語可追溯到英王喬治二世的聖誕大餐，但是戴紙帽可不能扣在這位十八世紀國王頭上，而是二十世紀初某個彩紙拉炮商想出的新玩意兒。

　　根據大英圖書館的檔案資料，國王和他的賓客收到了宴飲謎語——大概有幽默意味——讓他們在等待第一道菜時有點小消遣。這份聖誕節菜單十分燒腦費解，菜餚包括了「飾有九旬老婦的鳥屋」，據說是道湯品；「羅馬保護區碎片餡餅」；「冒牌貨的耳環燉菜」；「不安分的肢體剁碎混和理智，囚禁在朝臣的承諾中」，配菜則是「燒過的笑話重擊」。

　　笑鬧的興致還沒完，聖誕節隔天（Boxing Day）顯然也是玩笑謎語滿載的一天，包括「烤鼻煙壺內部」、「泅游在牛血和印度粉中的三頭龍」和「一盤子牛津學者」之類的菜餚。

　　看來過去兩百五十年雖然聖誕節的菜色有所進步，笑話的質量卻沒有。

LE MAITRE D'HOTEL FRANÇAIS.

TABLE DE S. A. R. LE PRINCE RÉGENT,

Servie au pavillon de Brighton, Angleterre, 16 Janvier 1817. Menu de 36 entrées.

HUIT POTAGES.

Le potage à la Condé,
Les nouilles à la Napolitaine,
La julienne au blond de veau,
La bisque d'écrevisses au blanc de volaille,

Le potage de santé, consommé de volaille;
Le potage de perdrix au chasseur,
Le potage à la Hollandaise,
L'orge perlée à la Russe.

HUIT RELEVÉS DE POISSONS.

La hure d'esturgeon au vin de Champagne,
Le gros brochet à la Chambord moderne,
Le turbot à la Hollandaise,
Les tronçons d'anguilles à l'Italienne,

Les perches à la Vaterfisch,
Le saumon à la Vénitienne,
Les soles à l'Anglaise, sauce aux huîtres,
Le cabillaud à l'Anglaise, sauce aux homards.

QUATRE GROSSES PIÈCES.

Le dinde aux truffes à la Périgord,
La pièce de bœuf à la cuillère,

Le quartier de veau à la Monglas,
Les faisans à la moderne.

TRENTE-SIX ENTRÉES, DONT QUATRE POUR LES CONTRE-FLANCS.

1. Les escalopes de perdreaux à la Périgord,
2. Les côtelettes de porc frais à la sauce Robert,
3*. Les petis vols-au-vent à la reine,
4. Le fritot de poulets à la tomate,
5. L'émincé de gibier garni de croûtons farcis.

LE GROS BROCHET A LA CHAMBORD.

6. Les filets de gélinottes au chasseur,
7**. La côte de bœuf à la gelée,
8. Les quenelles de volaille à l'Italienne,
9. Le sauté de pigeons à la Toulouse.

LE TURBOT A LA HOLLANDAISE.

10. Les escalopes de ris d'agneaux aux fines herbes,
11. Les filets de moutons à la Conti,
12**. La salade de homards aux laitues,
13. Le sauté de poulardes aux pointes d'asperges.

LES TRONÇONS D'ANGUILLES A L'ITALIENNE.

14. Les filets de faisans à la Pompadour,
15. Les poulets dépecés à la Vénitienne,
16*. Le pâté de lapereaux à l'ancienne,
17. Les papillottes de mauviettes à la Duxelle,
18. Les filets de volaille en damier.

18. Les filets de poulardes à la Chevalier,
17. Les côtelettes de veau à la Polonaise,
16*. La croustade de cailles au gratin,
15. Les ailerons de poulardes à la Macédoine,
14. Le hachis de faisans garni d'œufs pochés.

LES PERCHES A LA WATERFISCH.

13. Les filets de poulardes soufflés au suprême,
12**. Le pain de levrauts à la pelée,
11. Les caisses de foies gras à la Monglas,
10. La fricassée de poulets aux champignons.

LE SAUMON A LA VÉNITIENNE.

9. Le turban de palais de bœufs aux truffes,
8. Les boudins de perdreaux à la Richelieu,
7**. La blanquette de volaille à la magnonaise,
6. Les bécasses à la financière, entrée de broche.

LES SOLES A L'ANGLAISE.

5. Les filets de lapereaux en lorgnettes,
4*. Les côtelettes de mouton glacés, purée de navets;
3. Les petits pâtés à la Russe,
2. Les petits canetons de poulets à la Macédoine,
1. Les aiguillettes de canards à l'orange.

POUR EXTRA, DIX ASSIETTES VOLANTES DE FRITURE.

4. De laitances de carpes à la Harly,
4. De filets mignons panés à l'Anglaise,

2. De filets de perdreaux.

HUIT GROSSES PIÈCES D'ENTREMETS.

Le casque à la Romaine,
Le trophée de marine,
La dinde en galantine sur un socle,
La pyramide de p. de terre à la gelée, à l'Anglaise;

Le palmier aux boucliers,
Le casque à la grecque,
Le signe de saindoux dans une île,
Le jambon gelé sur un socle.

QUATRE PLATS DE ROTS.

Les faisans piqués,
Les poulets à la reine,

Les poulardes à l'Anglaise, sauce aux œufs;
Les gelinottes bardées.

TRENTE-DEUX ENTREMETS.

1. Les champignons grillés, demi-glace;
2**. La gelée de marasquins fouettée,
3. Les pommes de terre frites à la Lyonnaise.

LA GALANTINE SUR UN SOCLE.

4. Les truffes à l'Italienne,
5*. Les gâteaux glacés à la crème au café.

LES FAISANS PIQUÉS.

6*. Les madelaines au cédrat confies,
7**. La gelée de champignons rosée,
8. Les œufs pochés à la chicorée.

LE CASQUE ROMAIN.

9. Les salsifis à la Magnonaise,
10**. La gelée d'orange à la belle vue,
11*. Les marrons d'abricots glacés.

LES POULETS A LA REINE.

12*. Les diadèmes au gros sucre,
13. Les truffes à la serviette.

LA PIRAMYDE DE POMMES DE TERRE A LA GELÉE.

14. Le céleri à la Française,
15**. Le blanc-manger aux noix,
16. Les scakls ou choux de mer au beurre.

16. Les cardes à l'Espagnole,
15**. La crème au caramel, au bain-marie;
14. Les truffes au vin de Champagne.

LE CYGNE DE SAINDOUX DANS UNE ÎLE.

13. Les épinards à l'essence et en croustade.
12*. Les gaufres à la Parisienne.

LES CHAPONS A L'ANGLAISE.

11*. Les choux à la crème de vanille,
10**. La gelée d'ananas garnie,
9. La salade à l'Italienne.

LE CASQUE A LA GRECQUE.

8. Les œufs à l'aurore,
7**. La gelée d'épines-vinettes moulée,
6*. Les fanchonnettes à l'orange.

LES GELINOTTES.

5*. Les gâteaux renversés garnis de groseille,
4. Les navets à la Béchamel.

LE JAMBON SUR UN SOCLE.

3. Les truffes à la Périgueux,
2. Le fromage bavarois aux framboises,
1. Les laitues à l'essence de jambon.

POUR EXTRA, SIX ASSIETTES VOLANTES.

Les soufflés en croustade à l'orange, au cédrat, au marasquin, aux avelines.

一八一七年，卡漢姆的攝政晚宴菜單

1817

卡漢姆的攝政晚宴

　　將卡漢姆（Marie-Antoine Carême）尊為法國烹飪界教父絕非過譽，做為名廚文化的先驅，他從廚房雜工一路力求上進成為英王喬治四世登基前的私人廚師，並在聲望極高的巴黎糕點師傅拜伊（Sylvain Bailly）指導下接受法式糕點訓練。卡漢姆出師後開設了自己的和平街糕點鋪（Pâtisserie de la rue de la Paix），憑藉著美麗的糕點塔裝置藝術（pièces montées）開始闖出響亮名聲。琳瑯滿目的甜點如杏仁蛋白膏、糖果、牛軋糖、軟糖糖霜和蛋糕放在風格時尚的店鋪櫥窗裡，也陳列在巴黎富豪客戶的宴會中，就連拿破崙（Napoleon Bonaparte）都是他的顧客。

　　與這位法國領袖的往來使卡漢姆的重心轉往專業烹飪，並成為法國外交官塔列蘭－佩里戈爾（Charles Maurice de Talleyrand-Périgord）的私人廚師。塔列蘭－佩里戈爾對卡漢姆提出挑戰，想請他創造一整年分的當季菜單，菜色不得重複。完成這項特訓的獎賞是成為塔列蘭－佩里戈爾的廚房主廚，而其中某幾道菜餚今日仍在向來以簡潔優雅聞名的法式料理風格中占有重要地位。卸除主廚職務後，卡漢姆旅居俄羅斯、奧地利和英國，並成為英國攝政王喬治四世（George IV）的廚師。喬治四世當時出了名地熱愛美食，他顯然在維也納進行國是訪問期間品嘗過卡漢姆的手藝。

　　左頁菜單取自攝政王在布萊頓英皇閣（the Brighton Pavilion）舉行的晚宴，展現了卡漢姆的招牌風格：威尼斯鮭魚、鯪魚淋荷蘭醬與義大利風沙拉，再搭配他出色的天才型擺盤。卡漢姆八個月後就離職的原因尚不清楚，但一般認為是因為他討厭英國的氣候和食物。

攝政王在布萊頓英皇閣的用餐室

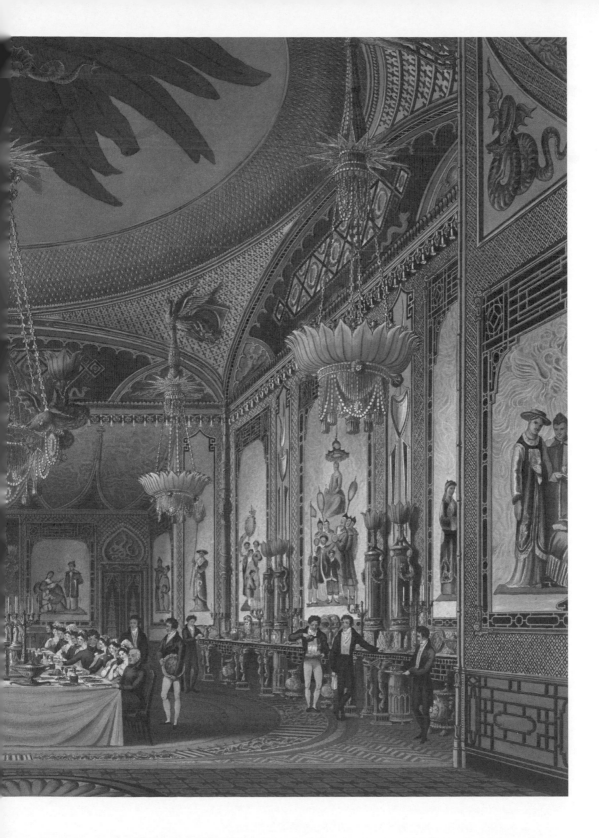

一八三九年發表的《小獵犬號航海記》中的美洲獅素描

一八三九年發表的《小獵犬號航海記》中的加拉帕戈斯海鬣蜥素描

1828

達爾文的饕客俱樂部

鷹
·
鸕鶿
·
灰林鴞

　　達爾文當然是因為演化論而聲名大噪，但他性格裡的另一面同樣留有紀錄——他是個吃貨。

　　一八二八年，達爾文放棄在愛丁堡的醫學學位，轉到劍橋大學攻讀神學學位，希望畢業後成為牧師。有鑑於他未來的成就，不免讓人猜測，達爾文很可能大學時就組過能夠反映這種熱愛大自然傾向的社團。這樣說不算錯，但完全不是你想的那樣。

　　達爾文和朋友創立了「饕客俱樂部」（'Glutton Club'），唯一目的是食用人們還不熟悉或尚未開發入菜的肉類。據說進入他們肚子裡的包括一隻鷹、一隻長得像蒼鷺的鸕鶿，以及一隻特別難吃的灰林鴞——有研究報告指出，這個大膽吃貨俱樂部因為這隻鴞而畫上句點。

　　還是學生的達爾文能嘗鮮的肉類選擇有限，但這種熱情一直延續到他後半生。從加拉帕戈斯群島的鬣蜥到犰狳和美洲獅，他吃了各種肉食。最有名的一頓飯是一頭重達九公斤的囓齒類動物，稱為刺鼠，他宣稱是「我所吃過最美味的肉」。

Jackson's admirers thought that every honor which Jefferson had ever received should be paid him, so some of them, residing in a rural district of New York, got up, under the superintendence of a Mr. Meacham, a mammoth cheese for " Old Hickory." After having been exhibited at New York, Philadelphia, and Baltimore, it was kept for some time in the vestibule at the

THE GREAT CHEESE LEVEE.

White House, and was finally cut at an afternoon reception on the 22d of February, 1837. For hours did a crowd of men, women, and boys hack at the cheese, many taking large hunks of it away with them. When they commenced, the cheese weighed one thousand four hundred pounds, and only a small piece was saved for the President's use. The air was redolent with cheese, the carpet was slippery with cheese, and nothing else

出自《佩利回憶錄》（*Perley's Reminiscence*）的插圖
〈超大起司壇〉（'The Great Cheese Levee'）

1837

傑克遜總統的大起司派對

紐約州的陳年巧達起司
·
威士忌

　　儘管聽起來不太像真的，但歐巴馬的「大起司日」（Big Block of Cheese Day）——與總統的高級幕僚在線上交流，任何想問政府的問題都可藉機尋求解答——實際上可追溯到美國前總統傑克遜（Andrew Jackson）一八三七年發起的活動。

　　傑克遜第二次總統任期結束前兩年，紐約州奧斯威戈村（Oswego）農民麥克漢姆（Thomas S. Meecham）據說為了表現自己更勝一籌，送了一個重達六百六十公斤的起司給總統——一八〇二年，某位麻薩諸塞州的農民送了重達三百四十公斤的起司給傑佛遜總統（Thomas Jefferson）。傑克遜總統盡可能分贈給朋友和幕僚後，決定在他任內最後一次白宮開放日分送起司給大家品嘗。根據紀錄，大約有一萬名群眾前來。儘管大起司很快就被處理完畢了，氣味卻顯然直到下一任總統范布倫（Martin Van Buren）還久久不散。

　　傑克遜的起司派對曾在一九九九年首播的美國電視影集《白宮風雲》（The West Wing）中出現，從此被永久記住。看來他受人民愛戴的好名聲如此牢固，起司的黏合功不可沒。

這幅插畫呈現巴黎圍城時期人們射殺動物園動物的情景

1870

巴黎圍城時期的聖誕大餐

驢頭塞奶油裹蘿蔔

·

象肉豆子湯

·

燉袋鼠

·

狼肉配鹿肉醬汁

從一八七〇年七月到一八七一年一月僅僅持續六個月的普法戰爭見證了巴黎圍城如何導致法國皇帝拿破崙三世（Emperor Napoleon III）垮臺，德意志帝國擴張，以及被稱為巴黎公社的社會主義政府在城市中崛起。普魯士軍隊封鎖了通往首都的所有公路和鐵路，試圖以切斷糧食供應迫使巴黎人民投降。令敵人吃驚的是，巴黎人仍然努力費了一番心思，做出了犧牲才願意認輸放棄。這座城市的居民真的吃掉了所有可利用的動物，這麼說一點也不誇張。

九月十八日被正式斷糧後，巴黎市民在頭兩個月繼續吃牛肉、羊肉、豬肉和魚，進入十月，菜單上出現了馬肉。一個月後的十一月，「家戶食用肉類」限量配額為每天一百克。不久，人們開始吃老鼠、貓和狗。

儘管對多數人都是極困頓難熬的日子，圍城第九十九天（正好是聖誕節）卻有一場盛宴。這滿盈著肉類的一餐很可能是犧牲巴黎動物園換來的。芳鄰餐廳（Voisin restaurant）為顧客提供六道式套餐，其中包括驢頭塞奶油裹蘿蔔、象肉豆子湯、燉袋鼠和狼肉配鹿肉醬汁。當這座城市於一個月後淪陷，落入普魯士軍隊掌控時，城裡已找不到任何動物足跡。

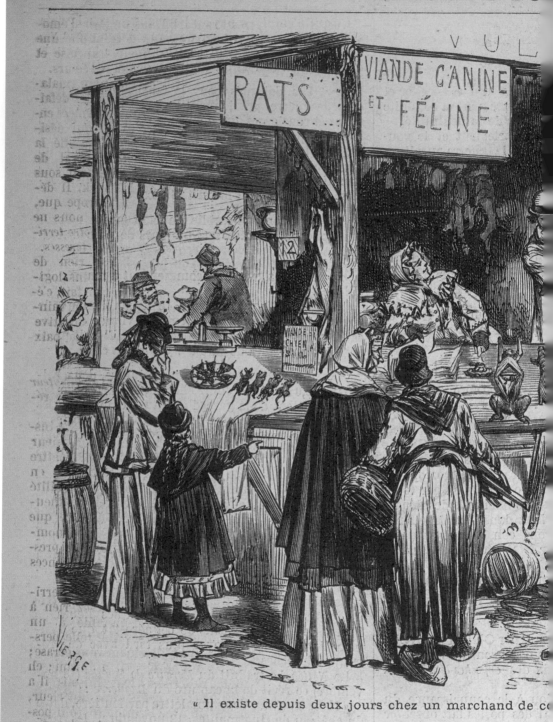

« Il existe depuis deux jours chez un marchand de cc

刻畫巴黎圍城時期的插畫，可看見屠夫在賣狗肉與貓肉

omestibles un étalage de viandes insolités (Voir page 150.)

沙皇某一次慶祝餐宴的菜單

1896

末代沙皇的鋪張盛宴

羅宋湯

·

俄式肉餡餃子

·

清蒸魚

·

羔羊排

·

冰淇淋

羅曼諾夫家族（Romanov）是一九一七年二月革命發生前統治俄羅斯的
最後一個王朝，關於這家人與其豪奢行徑的記載相當多。不管是在聖彼得堡
冬宮舉行持續兩天舞會所穿的華美服飾，還是精巧細緻、得就近在毗鄰宮殿
建築中備好料理的餐宴（一九〇二年還為此建造了一條隧道，以更有效的方
式運送菜色多樣的餐點），對細節的講究都是首要之務。有些古怪的沙皇尼
古拉二世（Tsar Nicholas II）據說對於飲食並不特別挑剔，但從他一八九六
年五月二十六日加冕典禮的菜單看來，桌子與菜單本身肯定還是必須符合該
有的排場。

左頁菜單的美術設計出自藝術家瓦斯涅佐夫（Viktor Vasnetsov）之手，
這位藝術家在十九世紀後期俄國復興運動（Russian Revivalist movement）中
占有重要地位。從菜單中可看到，新任沙皇盡情享用了傳統的羅宋湯、清蒸
魚、羔羊排、俄式肉餡餃子，餐後點心是冰淇淋。晚宴在加冕典禮隔天舉
行，沙皇也為前來宮殿慶祝的莫斯科市民提供了簡單的食物。然而，這場盛
會卻以災難告終，發生了人群踩踏事件，據說造成約三千人喪生，這起悲劇
標誌了三百年的羅曼諾夫王朝開始步向衰亡。

上圖與次頁：描繪加冕大典的插圖

一九六七年，貓王夫婦一起切結婚蛋糕

1967

貓王艾維斯與普里希拉的早餐婚宴

洛克菲勒焗烤生蠔

·

烤乳豬

·

炸雞

·

香檳

·

結婚蛋糕

　　一九五九年於西德相識，貓王艾維斯（Elvis Presley）與普里希拉・鮑利爾（Priscilla Beaulieu）談戀愛的時間長得驚人——事實上長達八年，男方直到一九六六年十二月才在他位於雅園（Graceland）的住處求婚。普里斯萊夫妻等到在拉斯維加斯舉行婚禮後才對外公開喜訊，並邀請攝影記者參加新婚夫婦為一百位親朋好友舉辦的早餐婚宴。

　　新人切下高達五英尺六層蛋糕的畫面無疑是這場活動中最讓人眼熟的影像，而以杏桃果醬、巴伐利亞奶油和摻了櫻桃白蘭地的糖霜調味，覆有軟糖花朵、窗格裝飾、婚禮鈴鐺和銀樹葉的結婚蛋糕並不算搶盡風采，比較像是起個頭的花絮。這頓早餐婚宴據說花了約一萬美元（按今日幣值計算約為八萬美元），採自助式供餐，既奢侈高級，又囊括了美國各地的經典家鄉味：烤乳豬、洛克菲勒焗烤生蠔（oysters Rockefeller）、龍蝦和炸雞，全部搭配無限暢飲的香檳。

　　不過，最能讓人聯想到貓王的知名食物可能是花生醬、培根和香蕉組成的三明治，就是所謂的「傻瓜黃金麵包條」（'Fool's Gold Loaf'）——在挖空的長條麵包裡塞滿花生醬、果醬，當然還有培根。婚禮當天以形象高雅為最高準則，因此很容易理解為什麼婚宴菜單上沒有這一道餐點。

一九〇二年，臭名昭彰的薩維奇俱樂部晚餐菜單

藝術中的美食

有些舉世仰望的藝術家、音樂家和作家似乎不只單憑他們揮灑創意的成果建立聲譽。若想知道著名爵士音樂家在演出後吃些什麼，或者文學精英有何用餐偏好，別猶豫，這一章就有你要的答案。

ROBERT BURNS

柏恩斯畫像與描繪他出生地的圖畫

1801

柏恩斯夜宴的起源

肉餡羊肚包

·

馬鈴薯泥和蕪菁甘藍泥

·

羊頭

　　蘇格蘭的傳統節日「柏恩斯之夜」（Burns Night）每年一月二十五日在全球各地都有慶祝活動，但很少有人知道與它相關的第一頓晚餐是在夏天中旬——七月二十一日舉行，就是詩人羅伯·柏恩斯（Robert Burns）逝世周年，該活動是為了紀念他而舉辦。

　　儘管各地柏恩斯夜宴（Burns suppers）的長度和形式可能有所不同，但有三樣東西是不變的：肉餡羊肚包、威士忌與讚美肉餡羊肚包的詩歌朗誦。晚宴最初在蘇格蘭艾爾郡（Ayrshire）阿洛維（Alloway）舉行，與吟遊詩人最親密的九個朋友聚在一起，向詩人與他的成就致敬。根據傳說，當時的活動非常有趣，因此與會者決定將它訂為一年一度的活動，後來才將慶祝活動改到一月柏恩斯生日那天。

SAVAGES AT THE ALBERT HALL.

THE BUFFALO DANCE AT THE ALBERT HALL
(FROM "THE GRAPHIC")

To face page 232

這幅插畫描繪了薩維奇俱樂部成員在皇家阿爾伯特音樂廳的薩維奇舞會上跳野牛舞
次頁：一九〇六年四月二十八日，薩維奇俱樂部會員晚宴菜單，伍德（Lawson Wood）的插畫作品

1883

皇家阿爾伯特音樂廳的
薩維奇俱樂部舞會

香檳
·
雪利酒
·
干邑白蘭地
·
黑咖啡

　　一八五七年在倫敦成立的薩維奇俱樂部（Savage Club）是英國最知名
的私人紳士俱樂部之一，成員集合了文壇名人、藝術家和音樂家，並提供了
一個比嘉禮客俱樂部（Garrick Club）更具波西米亞風格的選擇。

　　薩維奇俱樂部之名來自詩人理查·薩維奇（Richard Savage），就是詹
森（Samuel Johnson）《薩維奇傳記》（*The Life of Savage*）一書主角，至今
依然營運。知名成員包括馬克·吐溫（Mark Twain）、詹姆斯·貝瑞（J. M.
Barrie）、毛姆（W. Somerset Maugham）和狄倫·湯瑪斯（Dylan Thomas）。

　　除了在高雅藝文方面的突出地位，一八八三年七月，俱樂部假皇家阿爾
伯特音樂廳（the Royal Albert Hall）籌辦舞會，成為音樂廳自一八七一年三
月開放後，十二年來的第一場舞會。活動用意是要為皇家音樂學院吸引更
多贊助，包括威爾斯親王和王妃（Edward VII, Prince of Wales and Alexandra,
Princess of Wales）在內的與會賓客都能享用餐點和飲料 —— 至少有雪利酒、
干邑白蘭地、黑咖啡和香檳。隨後是深夜登場的野牛舞表演，這是北美原住
民的傳統儀式，由俱樂部成員穿著模仿傳統服飾的裝束登臺主演。薩維奇俱
樂部以舉辦高調又有些古怪的晚宴而聞名，總是伴隨著娛樂活動，並配上插
圖精美的菜單卡。

〈密碼與破解它的人〉（'The Cipher and the Man Who Solved It'），這是一九一四年《岸濱雜誌》（*The Strand Magazine*）九月號連載刊登的《恐怖谷》（*The Valley of Fear*）插圖

與王爾德和柯南・道爾
一起在朗廷酒店用餐

威尼斯風比目魚排／牛肋排配約克郡布丁
・
法式焗烤馬鈴薯／開心果冰淇淋

　　倫敦市內馬里波恩區的朗廷酒店（The Langham）吸引了許多尊貴有名的賓客光臨，身為歐洲第一家「豪華」飯店，其地位之高貴，威爾斯親王甚至於一八六五年親自蒞臨酒店開幕典禮。朗廷酒店享有此一殊榮的原因在於具備了許多創新的先進工業技術，包括液壓電梯、電燈和抽水馬桶等，再加上其他豪華裝潢，更不用說在這兒往來的都是名流顯要了。

　　事實上，一八七〇年巴黎圍城期間，拿破崙三世就住在朗廷酒店，這裡也是狄更斯、馬克・吐溫、諾爾・寇威爾（Noël Coward）和華莉絲・辛普森（Wallis Simpson）的最愛。不過最有名的忠實顧客或許是創造福爾摩斯的柯南・道爾爵士（Sir Arthur Conan Doyle），大作家甚至把〈波西米亞醜聞〉（"A Scandal in Bohemia"）和《四簽名》（*The Sign of Four*）部分場景設定在這裡。

　　《四簽名》背後其實有段小祕史。一八八九年夏天，柯南・道爾與出版代理商史陶達（J. M. Stoddart）一同用餐，討論為《利平科特月刊》（*Lippincott's Monthly Magazine*）供稿的事。後來，另一位嘉賓王爾德（Oscar Wilde）也加入了，兩人在晚餐中約定要為史陶達寫一個短篇故事。這兩篇作品後來發展成柯南・道爾的《四簽名》，以及堪稱王爾德最具影響力的作品《格雷的畫像》（*The Picture of Dorian Gray*）。

　　儘管他們那天吃了什麼並無正式紀錄，但我們確實知道當時的菜單：威尼斯風比目魚排、牛肋排配約克郡布丁、法式焗烤馬鈴薯、精選起司盤和開心果冰淇淋。二〇一〇年，餐廳外牆上貼了一塊綠色牌匾來紀念這樁美事。二〇一四年，朗廷酒店重現了他們當時的晚餐菜單，以慶祝這重大事件。

一八九九年，畢卡索為四隻貓餐館畫的菜單封面

畢卡索在巴塞隆納的出沒地點

馬鈴薯烘蛋配蒜泥蛋黃醬
·
加泰隆尼亞香腸和豆子

大家都知道畢卡索（Pablo Picasso）是位美食鑑賞家，他對所有可食用之物的描繪作品二〇一八年巡迴歐洲展出時，西班牙名廚阿德里亞（Ferran Adrià）等人都對這位藝術家的作品和胃口表示敬意。但，這一切是從哪裡開始的呢？

答案見仁見智，也許是位於巴塞隆納聲名狼藉哥德區的四隻貓餐館（Els Quatre Gats）。現代主義運動方興未艾之際，這家餐廳成了藝術家聚會的場所，十七歲的畢卡索搬到這座城市時，每天晚上都混在這裡的人群之中。四隻貓餐館的後廳有酒吧和卡巴萊歌舞秀（cabaret performances），氣氛相當熱絡，又帶有波西米亞風格，深受畢卡索喜愛，他甚至在這裡舉辦首次個展，展出二十五幅炭筆和水彩畫作品，還為菜單畫圖。

據說畢卡索偏好口味清淡的餐點，喜愛風格樸實、新鮮當季的在地美食，不喜歡花俏的東西。談起自己和第一任妻子愛好的口味，他說：「奧爾加（Olga）喜歡蛋糕和魚子醬，我喜歡加泰隆尼亞香腸和豆子。」很多時候，這位年輕的藝術家會在這樣一頓晚餐後拍賣自己的素描作品。儘管往後的經濟狀況有所改善，畢卡索的飲食喜好仍然很樸素。一九六四年接受《時尚》雜誌（Vogue）採訪時，他宣稱自己這輩子最喜歡的餐點是西班牙馬鈴薯烘蛋搭配蒜泥蛋黃醬。

一九一四年，詩人們在布朗特的房子外面合照

1914

當時詩人們吃孔雀當晚餐

烤牛肉

·

炙燒孔雀

　　藝文界曾有一次影響深遠的集會，匯聚了詩人龐德（Ezra Pound）、葉慈（W. B. Yeats）和名氣略遜的維克多·普拉（Victor Plarr）、托馬斯·摩爾（Thomas Sturge Moore）、理查·奧丁頓（Richard Aldington）和法蘭克·福林特（Frank Flint）。這些人聚集在威爾弗里德·布朗特（Wilfrid Scawen Blunt）薩塞克斯郡鄉村的家中，但他們吃這頓飯時沒有撕麵包，而是烤了孔雀。

　　這次聚會是應龐德的要求而辦的，他打算在與葉慈同住並擔任其祕書這段時間與英格蘭每位詩人碰面。布朗特本人也是詩人，妻子則是已故拜倫勳爵（Lord Byron）孫女安妮·拜倫（Lady Anne Isabella Noel Byron）。在葉慈的密友兼贊助人格雷果里夫人（Lady Gregory）的請求下，這隻鳥在上菜時是連同牠最有代表性的羽毛一同送上的，而且安排在比較安全的烤牛肉主餐之後。

　　詩人們於餐後合影留念，這張照片隨後不久便在英國、愛爾蘭和美國的報紙上引發了騷動。布朗特算是當時頗有聲望的社交主持人，而且隨著人們愈來愈關注「名流」藝術家，這類集會往往也被大書特書，獲得廣泛的報導。其中一次甚至成了傳說——據傳龐德有次在倫敦的老赤郡起司酒吧（Ye Old Cheshire Cheese）喝酒時，一邊討論自己的作品，一邊吃了一束鬱金香。

　　沒有任何報導指出詩人們如何評價這頓孔雀飯，但為了回禮，詩人們送了個手工雕刻的小石盒給主人布朗特，每個人都在盒中放入最新的作品。

海明威在密西根州沃倫湖（Walloon Lake）與自己捕到的魚合影，照片日期不明

1920

海明威的煎鱒魚與鬆餅

鬆餅淋蘋果奶油和肉桂糖漿

·

培根油煎鱒魚

　　海明威對美食的熱愛是出了名的 ——《流動的饗宴》（*A Moveable Feast*）
常被認為是獨樹一幟的城市指南，帶著讀者在巴黎穿街走巷之外，還有二十
世紀最有名的藝術家和作家隨行同逛餐館和酒吧。海明威也是位出色的戶外
活動玩家，對於蠅釣和露營的熱情完全不輸給在城裡走跳。他為加拿大報紙
《多倫多星周報》（*Toronto Star Weekly*）撰寫了一系列專欄，其中有些短
篇小說的靈感就來自野營旅行，年輕作家在其中一篇文章裡大加讚揚露宿野
外一兩個星期的好處。

　　根據海明威的說法，任何愉快的野營假期必不可少的就是食物，深信
「大多數露營行程都毀在烹飪」。為了解決這個常見的問題，他提供了詳細
的食譜並建議準備一個隨時可用的煎鍋，因為有淋上蘋果奶油和肉桂糖漿的
鬆餅，在烹調鱒魚時「大家就不會餓肚子」。此外，烹調時要用培根脂肪塗
鱒魚，並確保魚肉煮熟。最後，他宣稱：「如果說有比這種組合更棒的食
物，那在筆者孜孜矻矻致力於飲食的一生中還沒有嘗過。」如果這就是海明
威每次旅行時的美食標準，那還有什麼好說的？我們又能找誰爭辯呢？

一九四六年，艾靈頓公爵在紐約登臺演出的情況

1944

艾靈頓公爵與他的三十二份熱狗

紅茶
·
碎麥麩
·
三十二份熱狗

美國作曲家暨音樂人艾靈頓公爵（Duke Ellington）是爵士樂界的傳奇人物。一九二〇年代與一九三〇年代，他和他的樂隊經常在曼哈頓下城區和哈林區的爵士俱樂部演出，一九二七年至一九七四年間則陸續錄製了上千張唱片，無庸置疑地為後來的許多爵士樂手開闢出一條路。儘管艾靈頓必定會先以他的音樂留名青史，但與他親近的人對他的回憶不僅止於音樂才華，還有對美食的熱愛。

想吃得健康養生時，艾靈頓會點麥麩片（shredded wheat）和紅茶，但儘管意圖如此之好，仍不敵他無與倫比的好胃口。他自己說：「我敢說我是全美國吃最多熱狗的人。〔緬因州老果林海灘餐廳（Old Orchard Beach Restaurant）〕有位華格納太太（Mrs. Wagner），她製作的烤麵包是全美國最好的。她拿出一個烤麵包，然後加一片洋蔥，然後是一個漢堡排，然後是一片番茄，接著是融化的起司，然後是另一個漢堡排，然後又一片洋蔥，更多起司，更多番茄，最後疊上另一片麵包。她的熱狗堡裡面包了兩條熱狗。我一個晚上就吞了三十二份。」

在緬因州最有歷史的海灘度假勝地之一，艾靈頓和他的樂團經常在鎮上的碼頭賭場（Pier Casino）和皇宮樂園（the Palace）演奏，因此把胃口養大了。胃口和音樂一樣傳奇的艾靈頓公爵將在當地被永遠傳誦。

一九五四年，《麥田捕手》初版封面

1953

沙林傑的周六燒烤

烤牛肉

·

甜派

一九五一年出版的《麥田捕手》（*The Catcher in the Rye*）可說是二十世紀最具影響力的作品之一，作者沙林傑（J. D. Salinger）不僅因為這部成長小說，也由於後來隱居新罕布夏州鄉村而聲名鵲起。小說主人翁考菲爾德在他一九四五年發表的短篇小說〈我瘋了〉（'I'm Crazy'）初次登場，但後來在《麥田捕手》現身才引起全世界關注，截至今日，這本書的全球銷量已超過七千萬冊。

根據一般大眾普遍相信、幾乎已成神話的傳言，沙林傑是刻意離開紐約文學界，自我「流放」到新罕布夏州的康沃爾小鎮。事實上正好相反，他不時參與社交活動，包括每周一次在佛蒙特州哈特蘭公理教會（Congregational Church of Hartland）的烤牛肉「周六晚宴」（'Saturday Supper'）。沙林傑總是早早抵達，坐得很靠近擺甜派點心的桌子。據說他總是安靜地坐著，整晚在他的線圈筆記本上寫東西。

理所當然，人們對於他創造的角色考菲爾德吃喝了什麼討論得更深入，考菲爾德在不怎麼順利的約會後吃的那一頓安慰自己的晚餐——烤乳酪三明治和麥芽牛奶——部落格寫手、作家和廚師都不停地復刻重現。

This picture depicts the site of Scott's Restaurant as it probably looked in the middle of the 17th Century — The Windmill in the background gave the name to Gt. Windmill Street which runs — — alongside Scott's Restaurant to-day — — —

Scott's

To the Librarian of the Corporation of London Guildhall, the Secretary of the London Society, the Secretary of the London Topographical Society, and the Officials of the British Museum, we express our best thanks for the great assistance given to us in drawing up this cover, including the " Story of Pickadilly " which can be read on the back page.

SCOTT'S RESTAURANT LIMITED
Coventry Street, London, W.1

一九六五年，史考特餐廳的菜單

伊恩・佛萊明：史考特餐廳行動

香檳
・
生蠔
・
乾馬丁尼

「用搖的，不要攪」（'SHAKEN, NOT STIRRED'）大概是電影史上最著名的臺詞之一。詹姆士・龐德這句流傳後世的話是有現實根源的 —— 確切地說，來自位於梅菲爾區（Mayfair）的史考特餐廳（Scott's）。這家著名的西倫敦海鮮餐廳於一八〇〇年代中期開業時只是間生蠔海鮮小屋，二十世紀發展成有錢人的熱門聚會場所，一九五〇年代、一九六〇年代則是作家伊恩・佛萊明（Ian Fleming）的最愛。

佛萊明仍在情報部門任職時經常光顧史考特餐廳，並因為二戰期間在此用餐而被懷疑是德國間諜，當時服務生聽到他講德語，通報了倫敦警察廳總部蘇格蘭場。其實他那時正在執行任務，試圖揪出內鬼。

佛萊明書中的虛構情報員同樣是位忠實顧客，史考特餐廳經常出現在小說中，兩人甚至喜歡坐同一個位子 —— 二樓右手邊的角落，從窗邊可俯臨路燈。除了新鮮的現剝牡蠣、香檳和高級海鮮，史考特餐廳也提供乾馬丁尼調酒，正是佛萊明 —— 與龐德 —— 喜歡的調酒。在《太空城》（Moonraker）中，當龐德計畫帶走瑪麗・古德奈，同樣明確提到了以這家餐廳做為約會之夜的地點。

WHITE STAR LINE.

R.M.S. "TITANIC."　　　　　APRIL 14, 1912.

THIRD CLASS.
BREAKFAST.
OATMEAL PORRIDGE & MILK
SMOKED HERRINGS, JACKET POTATOES
HAM & EGGS
FRESH BREAD & BUTTER
MARMALADE　　　SWEDISH BREAD
TEA　　　COFFEE

DINNER.
RICE SOUP
FRESH BREAD　　　CABIN BISCUITS
ROAST BEEF, BROWN GRAVY
SWEET CORN　　　BOILED POTATOES
PLUM PUDDING, SWEET SAUCE
FRUIT

TEA.
COLD MEAT
CHEESE　　　PICKLES
FRESH BREAD & BUTTER
STEWED FIGS & RICE
TEA

SUPPER.
GRUEL　　　CABIN BISCUITS　　　CHEESE

Any complaint respecting the Food supplied, want of attention or incivility, should be at once reported to the Purser or Chief Steward. For purposes of identification, each Steward wears a numbered badge on the arm.

鐵達尼號撞上冰山當天，船上三等艙乘客的菜單

最後一餐

「最後一餐」極適合做為最後一個章節，蒐集的範圍從空前絕後到精心策劃，從簡單樸實到十足古怪，統統都有。不論是著名餐廳的天鵝輓歌，還是惡名響亮的政治人物嚥下的最後一口，從地震天災到歷史轉折點，以下介紹的餐宴都為這一切留下了紀錄。

一八六四年，納斯特（Thomas Nast）為《哈潑周刊》（*Harper's Weekly*）
畫的插圖〈聯邦聖誕晚宴〉（'The Union Christmas Dinner'）

1864

林肯的最後一次聖誕晚宴

火雞

·

蛋奶酒

·

水果蛋糕

世上的領袖們總有無數關於他們如何張羅奢侈美饌、縱情享受飲食的傳說故事，美國總統林肯（Abraham Lincoln）卻是個口味簡單的人，簡單到早餐只用一杯咖啡打發，即使最豪華的晚餐最多也只有兩道菜。然而，一八六四年的聖誕節之所以如此重要有兩個原因：首先，喬治亞州薩凡納（Savannah）*被攻破，標誌了美國內戰即將結束；其次，這是林肯總統一八六五年四月十四日遇刺前，最後一次享用聖誕晚宴。

為了慶祝謝爾曼（William Tecumseh Sherman）將軍在南部的勝利，林肯下令聖誕節當天鳴放三百響禮炮致敬。配合突如其來的節日氣氛，林肯的小兒子塔德（Tad）邀請了一群當地報社記者參加。由於天氣寒冷，記者們既疲倦又饑餓。當時的菜單上肯定有火雞，還有蛋奶酒、橙子和水果蛋糕。那時候的聖誕節還不是美國的國定假日──那是五年後的事。

人們常說林肯沒什麼情調，但想想他的任期主要是美國內戰期間，多少可以理解慶祝活動為何如此低調。

---

*始建於一七三三年的薩凡納是喬治亞州最古老的城市。相傳在美國南北戰爭時期，北軍名將謝爾曼為了全面摧毀南軍士氣與恢復力，奉命不計一切代價，對南軍據點實施焦土戰術。他在徹底燒毀亞特蘭大（Atlanta）之後，決定向大海行軍，攻占薩凡納。沿途摧毀農田與住宅，破壞了一切工業設施及基礎建設。但當他拿下薩凡納後，卻決定維持這座美麗城市的原貌，做為贈送給林肯總統的耶誕禮物。

R.M.S. "TITANIC"

APRIL 14, 1912

FIRST CLASS DINNER

HORS D'OEUVRE VARIES

OYSTERS

CONSOMME OLGA   CREAM OF BARLEY

SALMON. MOUSSELINE SAUCE. CUCUMBER

FILET MIGNONS LILI

SAUTE OF CHICKEN LYONNAISE

VEGETABLE MARROW FARCIE

LAMB. MINT SAUCE

ROAST DUCKLING. APPLE SAUCE

SIRLOIN OF BEEF   CHATEAU POTATOES

GREEN PEAS   CREAMED CARROTS

BOILED RICE

PARMENTIER & BOILED NEW POTATOES

PUNCH ROMAINE

ROAST SQUAB & CRESS

RED BURGUNDY

COLD ASPARAGUS   VINAIGRETTE

PATE DE FOIE GRAS

CELERY

WALDORF PUDDING

PEACHES IN CHARTREUSE JELLY

CHOCOLATE & VANILLA ECLAIRS

FRENCH ICE CREAM

鐵達尼號頭等艙的菜單

1912

鐵達尼號上的最後一餐

　　皇家郵輪鐵達尼號（RMS Titanic）的頭等艙乘客也許吃了二十世紀最傳奇的一餐——也是他們的最後一餐。過去一百年中，這奢靡又歡樂的場景已被無數書籍和電影描述過。據說為了餵飽從頭等艙到三等艙的數千名乘客，船上廚房除了有十九個烤箱，一個專門為餐具而設的艙室，甚至還有類似肉舖和蔬菜雜貨店的地方。

　　唯一一份自鐵達尼號最後一夜救回並修復的菜單是頭等艙餐廳菜單，一頓晚餐裡提供十道菜以上，並搭配上等葡萄酒。在那宿命般的最後一餐當晚——一九一二年四月十四日午夜前，船撞上了冰山——打頭陣的是新鮮牡蠣，然後是清燉肉湯、鮭魚配慕斯淋醬、菲力牛排、烤小鴨佐蘋果醬汁、烤乳鴿、蘆筍冷盤和肥鵝肝餅，這只是其中幾道，餐末還有巧克力閃電泡芙、桃子果肉果凍和冰淇淋。

　　倖存的廚房工作人員中，最著名的也許是烘焙主廚賈克林（Charles Joughin）的故事。這位來自英國伯肯黑德（Birkenhead）的先生不僅為救生艇乘客備妥麵包，放棄了自己在最後一艘救生艇的座位，還奇蹟般地在海中踩水近三個小時後獲得救援。

拉斯普京的相片，拍攝日期不明

1916

拉斯普京嚥下最後一口

扎庫斯基

·

魚湯

·

蜂蜜蛋糕

做為俄羅斯沙皇尼古拉二世（Tsar Nicholas II）心靈上的夥伴，拉斯普京（Grigori Rasputin）的名氣主要來自他與羅曼諾夫家族關係匪淺的種種傳言，而非個人生活的確實事件，他的生平經歷鮮為人知。

拉斯普京後來被稱為「瘋狂僧侶」（'mad monk'），早年成長於西伯利亞，父母相當貧窮。儘管已經娶妻生子，他二十三歲那年卻在修道院裡有了一次精神上的覺醒。隨後幾年，他結識了俄羅斯東正教許多教會名人，最終於一九〇六年與羅曼諾夫家族碰面。到了第一次世界大戰時，拉斯普京已經成為沙皇妻子亞莉珊德拉（Alexandra）仰賴的精神導師，並照護醫治他們的兒子阿列克謝（Alexei），關於他的其餘故事就屬於傳說了。

若談到吃飯，傳記作者們對於拉斯普京的口味偏好眾說紛紜，像是他是否如傳言所云，像貴族一樣嗜食香檳和魚子醬，或者是他從小習慣的簡單飲食——黑麵包、根莖蔬菜和茶。不過，所有人都同意他熱愛葡萄酒，特別是馬德拉酒（Madeira），以及他的餐桌禮儀非常糟糕——他在吃東西時會舔手指，鬍鬚經常沾黏食物。

有傳聞說，去世那天晚上，「瘋狂僧侶」拉斯普京吃了俄羅斯傳統開胃菜扎庫斯基（zakuski）和魚湯，然後被打算刺殺他的尤蘇波夫（Felix Yusupov）騙到家裡吃蜜糕——像往常一樣，邊吃邊喝大量的馬德拉酒。他的食物是否被下毒還不清楚，總之晚餐過後，他被槍殺並扔進了小涅瓦河（Malaya Nevka river）。短短兩個月後，羅曼諾夫王朝便被推翻了。

法魯克國王與他女兒菲莉婭爾公主（Farial）

1965

法魯克國王：埃及王朝最終章

生蠔
·
烤小羊排
·
蛋糕

　　從十六歲那年當上埃及國王開始，法魯克一世（Farouk I）終其一生都是極富爭議性的領導人。這個由英國創建的君主體制國家是相對較新的政權，法魯克是第十任國王，但他揮霍無度與放縱享樂的行徑——威士忌、美酒、佳餚，若傳言屬實的話，還有情色領帶收藏——使他被視為一個下流胚子和花花公子，而不是一位稱職的領袖。因此在掌權十六年後，這位國王被自家軍隊於一九五二年發動政變推翻也不足為奇。儘管法魯克的小兒子被宣布為埃及的新國王，他和家人仍逃到了義大利，最終定居摩納哥，在那裡繼續過著浮華的生活，直到一九六五年去世。

　　一如奢侈的生活方式，法魯克的死同樣深具戲劇性。這位前國王在羅馬的法蘭西島餐廳（Ile de France）與一名年輕女伴吃完生蠔、烤小羊排和蛋糕後，在抽雪茄時心臟病發，當場去世，享年四十五歲。

尼克森在白宮最後一頓午餐

1974

尼克森總統在白宮最後一頓午餐

茅屋起司與鳳梨

·

一杯牛奶

　　水門案的汙點讓尼克森（Richard Nixon）第二次入主白宮也許成了美國歷史上最受爭議的總統任期之一。當時人們發現，尼克森政府除了在位於華盛頓特區的民主黨全國委員會總部安裝竊聽器，還做出騷擾、打壓和宣誓後公然說謊等諸多政治不當的行為，近五十名官員因此遭到起訴。可想而知，這些消息損害了公眾對尼克森的信任，下臺命運已成定局。為了避免被彈劾，尼克森選擇於一九七四年八月九日進行全美電視直播，宣布辭職。

　　尼克森任內的標準餐點內容走的是美式家常風，如美式肉餅、冰淇淋聖代，但他辭職當天的午餐非常簡單：鳳梨、茅屋起司和一杯牛奶。不到二十四小時後，尼克森下臺，副總統福特（Gerald Ford）宣誓就職。雖然當時的白宮官方攝影師克努森（Robert Knudsen）平日並不會特別拍總統的餐點內容，卻拍下了這頓午飯。這張照片現在已經成為美國政府歷史上唯一一次總統辭職的悲慘寫照。

料理好準備上桌的圍鴉

1995

密特朗的天鵝輓歌

生蠔
·
鵝肝醬
·
閹雞
·
圃鵐

密特朗（François Mitterrand）既是法國第一位當選總統的社會主義者，也是任期最長的總統，任期從一九八一年持續到一九九五年。從政前的密特朗在二戰期間曾於法國軍隊服役，但被德軍俘虜並送進監禁營區，後來成功逃脫，於一九四三年加入反抗軍。隨後幾年，密特朗在社會黨的地位節節升高，最終成為法蘭西第五共和國的領袖。

這麼長的任期，密特朗不免經歷了一連串高低起伏，但他最後一場餐宴倒是概括了縱情吃喝之舉，這頓飯是一九九六年一月八日吃的，就在他因為前列腺癌病逝前幾天。

這餐飯的內容包括了生蠔、鵝肝醬、一隻閹雞和一隻稱為圃鵐的法國原生鳥類——某種據說象徵法國靈魂的小鳴禽。圃鵐固然是餐桌上的珍品，食用牠卻絕對是高度不合法的。自古以來，食用這種鳥的方式是用白布蓋住，然後整隻——包括頭、骨頭和所有部位——塞進嘴裡。圃鵐常常會被泡在雅瑪邑白蘭地的大酒桶中先行淹死，畢竟這種方式對雙方來說都比較容易接受。

鬥牛犬餐廳的員工進行前置準備

2011

鬥牛犬餐廳最後一次上菜

百香果「魚子醬」

·

甜／點

·

龍蝦羊腦沙拉

　　一九九〇和二〇〇〇年代分子料理的崛起有一部分功勞得歸功於西班牙廚師阿德里亞（Ferran Adrià）。這位鬥牛犬餐廳（El Bulli）的幕後功臣讓這家屢獲殊榮的創新餐廳獲得米其林三星，並登上無數「最佳餐廳」榜單。

　　位於西班牙加泰隆尼亞北部沿海玫瑰城（Roses）的鬥牛犬餐廳起初只是海灘酒吧，一九六一年到二〇一一年間則從簡單的供餐果腹之地轉變成飲食藝術的秀場。看看阿德里亞的學徒們，當今世界頂尖名廚師赫然在列：方濟會小酒館（Osteria Francescana）的博圖拉（Massimo Bottura）、Noma 的雷哲度（René Redzepi）、邊境橡樹餐廳（Mugaritz）的阿杜里茲（Andoni Luis Aduriz）和羅卡兄弟酒窖（El Celler de Can Roca）的璜·羅卡（Joan Roca），而這僅僅只是其中四人。

　　二〇一一年歇業前最後幾星期，鬥牛犬餐廳為記者、仕紳名流和死忠美食鐵粉舉辦了最後的晚宴，以紀念餐廳內一些最著名的菜餚，例如藉由反向晶球化作用做成的液態橄欖就是一道極具代表性的分子料理經典菜餚。

　　餐廳最後一次晚宴名為「最後的華爾滋」，當時有四十五位資深工作人員的家人和朋友參加，還有以前的學徒們。這頓飯有五十道菜，大部分內容保密，但根據報導，許多道菜都向餐廳過往的招牌菜致敬——百香果「魚子醬」、甜／點（Des／sert）、龍蝦羊腦沙拉——並以阿德里亞風格的梅爾芭蜜桃霜淇淋——畫下句點。最後這道是「新料理」（nouvelle cuisine）教父艾斯科菲耶發明的，贏得了如雷掌聲。這場聚會也一如大家所料地持續到了天明。

索引

文獻類

The last guest –

HISTORY 055

品菜單：令人垂涎的經濟與社會變革紀錄
THE MENU: Memorable Meals from Escoffier at the Ritz to a Suffragettes' Victory Dinner to the First Meal on the Moon

作　　者 — 伊芙·馬洛（Eve Marleau）
譯　　者 — 林柏宏
主　　編 — 邱憶伶
責任編輯 — 陳詠瑜
行銷企畫 — 林欣梅
封面設計 — FE 設計
內頁設計 — 張靜怡

編輯總監 — 蘇清霖
董 事 長 — 趙政岷
出 版 者 — 時報文化出版企業股份有限公司
　　　　　　108019 臺北市和平西路三段 240 號 3 樓
　　　　　　發行專線 —（02）2306-6842
　　　　　　讀者服務專線 — 0800-231-705・（02）2304-7103
　　　　　　讀者服務傳真 —（02）2304-6858
　　　　　　郵撥 — 19344724 時報文化出版公司
　　　　　　信箱 — 10899 臺北華江橋郵局第 99 號信箱
時報悅讀網 — http://www.readingtimes.com.tw
電子郵件信箱 — newstudy@readingtimes.com.tw
時報出版愛讀者粉絲團 — https://www.facebook.com/readingtimes.2

法律顧問 — 理律法律事務所　陳長文律師、李念祖律師
印　　刷 — 和楹印刷有限公司
初版一刷 — 2020 年 11 月 13 日
定　　價 — 新臺幣 460 元
（缺頁或破損的書，請寄回更換）

品菜單：令人垂涎的經濟與社會變革紀錄／伊芙·
馬洛（Eve Marleau）著；林柏宏譯 . -- 初版 . -- 臺
北市：時報文化，2020.11
　232 面；17×23 公分 . --（History；55）
　譯自：THE menu: memorable meals from escoffier
　　at the ritz to a suffragettes' victory dinner to
　　the first meal on the moon.

　ISBN 978-957-13-8412-2（平裝）

　1. 飲食風俗　2. 歷史

538.709　　　　　　　　　　　　109015712

ISBN　978-957-13-8412-2
Printed in Taiwan